Interracial Housing

Interracial Housing

A PSYCHOLOGICAL EVALUATION OF A SOCIAL EXPERIMENT

BY

MORTON DEUTSCH

AND

MARY EVANS COLLINS

Research Center for Human Relations
New York University

NEW YORK / RUSSELL & RUSSELL

GHETTO is an ugly word. It brings to mind images of people herded together behind barricades: people restricted and cut off.

But there are barricades in the United States restricting and confining Negroes, Mexicans, Orientals, and other segments of our population to ghettos which are as real as the walls that surrounded the Jews in Warsaw. They are intangible; they exist in the customs of society and in the minds of men. If they were made of more visible substance, perhaps, as Americans, we would be more aware of and thus more shocked by the ghettos in which more than 15 million fellow citizens are effectively segregated.

The walls of custom and belief which keep Negroes segregated from whites are not only a blot on our own national, democratic ideals but they are also a serious blow to our reputation among the nations. In a period of history when the United States is attempting to provide moral leadership for the nations throughout the world, many of whom have dark-skinned populations, the seriousness of the damage to our reputation cannot be overestimated. National self-interest, as well as moral precept, suggest the importance of eliminating the invisible barriers which shape our American ghettos.

The Field Foundation, believing in the importance of interracial and intercultural relations to a democratic society, has decided that one of its principal activities is to support research in this area. We believe that research can do much to hasten the process of outmoding prejudice. Already, the findings of anthropologists, biologists, psychologists, and other scientists have thrown into disrepute the doctrine of racial inferiority. It is no longer intellectually respectable to hold the racial beliefs which have been employed to justify prejudice. Research such as that reported in this book by Dr. Deutsch and Mrs. Collins should help us take the next step. By providing knowledge of the social and psychological effects of alternative social practices, it should provide a useful guide to citizens and public officials who wish to remove the blot of racial prejudice from the American scene.

A current development of great significance for the future of intergroup relations in America is the large-scale, government-supported building program now under way. With the aid of federal funds, approximately 810,000 low-rent dwelling units (five times as much public housing for low-income groups as there is today) can be constructed in the next few years by various Housing Authorities throughout the country. In addition, federal funds will be used to stimulate an extensive program of slum clearance or urban redevelopment. Furthermore, federal, state, and municipal governments will probably take increasing responsibility for the construction of dwelling units for low- and middle-income families both by actual building and by partial subsidization of building through urban redevelopment laws. It has been estimated that this government-initiated or government-stimulated housing will represent the major part of new housing construction for low-income families and a sizable proportion of new developments for urban middle-class families.

The decisions that are made for or against interracial occupancy in these public and semipublic housing developments will have major implications with respect to the future of residential segregation in the North and possibly in the entire United States. If Negro and white families are housed in separate developments, not only will new areas of segregation be established but also existing patterns of residential segregation will be strengthened through the moral support they receive from the new programs. If, on the other hand, the new developments are interracial, marked inroads will have been made upon our present ghettos. The time for decision is now.

The staff of the Research Center for Human Relations are to be commended for seizing the opportunity to study interracial housing. The results of their research into one of the most significant social experiments of our time should be a stimulus to further research in this area. It should also raise fundamental issues for discussion among housing officials and citizens throughout the country as they consider various policies with respect to the large-scale housing programs which are about to get under way. These decisions, as Dr. Deutsch and Mrs. Collins point out, have far-reaching implications for interracial relations in the United States and, as I have indicated, for our moral influence among the nations. They should not be made lightly and without knowledge of their implications.

The Field Foundation is happy to have helped to make this study available. It may be of great value to those who would replace superstition with science in making up their minds about interracial housing.

MARSHALL FIELD

July 1950

THIS book reports the first of a program of studies in intergroup relations being conducted by the staff of the Research Center for Human Relations. The focus of this program is upon the problem of pre-
dicting and controlling the human relations consequences of social
contact between persons from different racial and cultural groups. Experience shows that such contact may result either in friendlier attitudes and behavior or in an exaggeration of existing suspicions and
antagonisms. This becomes of increasing social importance as legal
and judicial action against the segregation of racial and cultural
groups brings together involuntarily great numbers of people who
otherwise would have avoided such association. A study of the conditions which favor friendly or unfriendly outcomes of intergroup
contact will be of value in attempts at practical prediction and control. At the same time such an effort will contribute to our understanding of the more general problem of the dynamics of attitude
and behavior change and derive its broader theoretical interest from
this fact.

The Research Center for Human Relations emphasizes in its research orientation several considerations which are well illustrated by
the study here reported.

The first of these is that our selection of research problems is
strongly influenced by judgments of social urgency. Our convictions
about the current significance for American society of intergroup relations and of interracial housing in particular led us to the questions
which Dr. Deutsch and Mrs. Collins investigated. Similar beliefs have
resulted in our choice of the other programs and projects we are attempting to carry out. This is not to say that other factors have no
impact upon our problem selection; we are, of course, influenced by
financial considerations, by the availability of research settings, by
the relationship of the problem to broader questions (in the case of
this study to the dynamics of attitude and behavior change), etc.
But within the limits prescribed by such factors and others like them,
we choose first for study those issues we believe to have social significance. The relation of this study to significant social issues has

vii

already been dramatically documented in the Postcript (see pages 130–31) by Mr. Danzig, Executive Director of the Newark Housing Authority. Mr. Danzig points out how the research reported in this book has helped to bring about a major change in housing policy in the city of Newark.

Our emphasis on socially significant problems is paralleled by an emphasis on a second consideration which this study also illustrates. We believe that research on such problems can be conducted in such a way as to achieve results which not only have immediate social consequences for the setting in which the research was conducted but also are generalizable to other settings. The achievement of social utility, in other words, carries no necessary implication that research results are less scientifically meaningful. The ability to generalize is, in socially useful, as in socially unuseful, research, primarily dependent on the proper use of familiar scientific procedures rather than on the nature of the research topic. To be sure, the use of certain procedures, such as precise controls, will not often be feasible in research conducted in community rather than laboratory settings. On the other hand, as this study illustrates, an approximation to the needed controls can often be made and when this is done generalizations of the sort Dr. Deutsch and Mrs. Collins propose are warranted.

This is not to deny, as the authors repeatedly point out, that some of their interpretations are based on assumptions for which they have no conclusive proof. Even under the best conditions, however, the most one can do at present in social research is to establish some degree of confidence in an interpretation. The degree of confidence will increase, as is the case in this study, if the findings are consistent with existing knowledge and theory; it will increase further if the findings are confirmed when the same problem is investigated under different social circumstances. This is why a replication of this study is currently being carried out.

The final point about the Research Center's general orientation which this study illustrates is that it is part of a series of interrelated studies in a research program whose focus has been noted above. Our experience with this program should contribute to the general experience with research planning and add to the empirical assessment of its promise for the acceleration of scientific progress at a time of great need.

STUART W. COOK
Director of Research, Research Center for
Human Relations, New York University

December 1950

THE significance of race relations to a democratic society has long been recognized by social scientists. Perhaps no other single area has been the subject of so much attention. Literally thousands of books, monographs, and articles have been devoted to problems of race relations. In view of the already existing voluminous literature, how can another study such as the present one be justified? By way of answer, it seems relevant to indicate that only a fraction of the time, money, and effort that has already been expended on the creation of atomic weapons has been spent on learning how to break down the barriers which separate group from group. Knowledge of the techniques which facilitate human cooperation is perhaps as socially important as knowledge of the techniques which enhance the power of human destruction.

Further, we agree with Lippitt and Radke, "The literature in this field, until very recently, shows a narrow emphasis on the surface aspects of the problem. . . . Descriptive data of a static variety constitute the major proportions: How many persons, what kind of persons, have prejudices against what kinds of objects or people? What is the content of the prejudices? To what sociological data (socio-economic level, age, sex, and so forth) can these prejudices be related? It is quite another matter to obtain an understanding of the dynamics of prejudice." [1] The simple fact is that there have been very few studies which have centered about changing prejudices. Most studies have been oriented toward the present or past rather than toward the future. They have been concerned with finding out what exists and how it has come to exist rather than in uncovering techniques for social change. Knowledge of the former, it may well be argued, is a necessary antecedent to the latter; even so, it is not a substitute.

In addition to the scarcity of studies in the reduction of prejudice,[2] most such studies have been limited to the investigation of influ-

[1] R. Lippitt and M. Radke, "New Trends in the Investigation of Prejudice," *Annals*, 244:167-76 (1946).

[2] For a good summary of such studies see A. Rose, *Studies in the Reduction of Prejudice*, American Council on Race Relations (1947).

ences (such as a college course, a motion picture, a visit to a Negro hospital) "which were probably relatively minor in relation to other influences in the subject's social milieu." [3] The often discouraging and inconclusive results of such investigations may well reflect the comparatively superficial nature of the influences being studied. The strength of the social and psychological barriers to democratic race relations as well as the pervasiveness of discrimination and prejudice suggest that a reduction in prejudices will require strong influences. The social scientist is rarely in the position where he, himself, has the opportunity to create these influences. He has neither the political power nor the financial resources to produce of his own accord a major social experiment. Nevertheless, social "experiments" are going on all the time; or perhaps more accurately, major attempts at producing social and psychological changes of one sort or another are a commonplace.

With the aid of scientific controls, the social scientist may occasionally be able to convert an attempt at social change into a social experiment. This is the purpose of our study. *We wish to investigate the effects upon prejudice of, perhaps, one of the most important "social experiments" in the area of race relations — the establishment of publicly supported nonsegregated interracial housing projects.* Unfortunately, as in most "social experiments," social scientists did not participate in the design of the "experiment." The problem we face, then, is to convert, *ex post facto*, a "social change" into a scientific "social experiment." The method by which we attempt to do this will be made clear in the body of the text.

Values to guide social research. As scientists have turned their methodology to an analysis of the process of science, it has become increasingly clear that the activities of the scientist are rarely, if ever, value-free. This is natural and inevitable since science is not something apart from society; it is shaped by and, at the same time, helps to shape the environment in which it must function. However, the environment in which scientists function in a democratic society does not present a uniform, undifferentiated, unvarying set of values which he must inevitably accept. There are various currents of opinion and diversified ideologies from which he may absorb or select values with which to guide his work. With no attempt to present an elaborate rationale, we wish to indicate briefly the value framework of the present study.

[3] R. M. Williams, Jr., *The Reduction of Intergroup Tensions*, Social Science Research Council Bulletin No. 57 (1947).

Being a *scientist*, adhering rigorously to the methods of scientific procedure, taking all precautions to prevent bias from influencing the collection, analysis, and presentation of data — these are, we believe, the first duties of the research worker. The problem of bias in research is not in any way unique to the social sciences; it arises as a possibility whenever there are preconceptions, personal motives, or social values which are relevant to the research outcome.[4] Since these factors are always present — otherwise there would be no motivation to do research — it is necessary for the research worker to adhere rigorously to the safeguards inherent in the methodology of his scientific discipline. We consider this to be a basic presupposition underlying all research.

Somewhat more controversial, undoubtedly, is our belief in the desirability of continuously being aware of the ultimate social justification for research. It is only on the assumption that social scientists will not shirk their social responsibilities that "not only the very considerable financial investment of society in their work, but the interferences in other people's affairs which are inevitably bound up with our research can be justified." [5] We believe, in other words, that the social scientists has a responsibility, not merely to further his own esthetic and intellectual pleasures in the course of research, but also to contribute to the solution of important social problems. Acceptance of such a responsibility has implicit within it an assumption (or hope) which runs counter to a fatalistic or laissez-faire interpretation of societal processes. It implies that informed effort, that action directed by knowledge, has the possibility of leading to desired social objectives.

This dynamic value premise (instead of the fatalistic or static one) has direct implications for theoretical as well as for applied social research. Recognizing the existing social customs and psychological beliefs concerning race relations, for example, and having a desire to change some of these in one direction or another, we should be interested in studying how customs and beliefs are maintained, the social structures which give them support, the exceptions to them and how these exceptions are initiated and stabilized, and the results of different attempts at changing them. A dynamic view calls for change ex-

[4] S. W. Cook's "The Role of Social Values in Social-Psychological Research," a paper presented at the American Psychological Association meetings in 1949, discusses these factors in detail.

[5] T. Parsons, "The Prospects of Sociological Theory," *American Sociological Review*, 15:3–15 (1950).

periments to reveal underlying processes; a static view is satisfied with correlational studies or studies of what exists.

An acceptance of social responsibility does not necessarily imply that all research must have immediate social usefulness. As Kurt Lewin has pointed out, in the long run "there is nothing so practical as a good theory," and it would be hazardous indeed to limit research to that which only has immediate usefulness. Nevertheless, frequently theory can be advanced equally well by any one of a number of alternative settings for research and, of course, when the research is intended to be immediately relevant to practical problems, the basic value premise has immediate implications for the formulation of the research problem. In such cases we believe *the research should be formulated so that it is strategically useful in facilitating democratic social change.*

To be socially useful, research must deal with problems that have present social consequences or that are likely to demand solution within the near future.[6] Further, from the point of view of producing change, knowledge about factors which we can do little about is less important than knowledge about factors which we can do a great deal about. "Somehow the impression has gotten about that research which traces phenomena such as prejudice back to their origins is more basic than other kinds of research and, therefore, more respectable. There is little reason for calling research on factors which sustain and maintain prejudice any less basic than the genetic type of research. The only difference is that the second type of research is more likely to yield useful information than the first." [7]

To be used, social research must seem relevant to important social decisions in-the-making. For this to happen, it is probable that the decision-makers must be directly or indirectly involved in the study in order to enlist their interest and to forestall resistance (this is the rationale for "action research"), and the study must appear in a context which the decision-makers can readily see is directly related to their as yet unmade decisions.

We have stressed the function of social research in facilitating social change but neither as social scientists nor as citizens do we wish to facilitate change independently of its nature. We are interested in changes which decrease rather than increase the discrepancy between our social ideals and social reality. As a normative standard we are

[6] For a fuller discussion of some of these points see C. Selltiz and S. W. Cook, "Can Research in Social Science Be Both Socially Useful and Scientifically Meaningful," *American Sociological Review*, 13:454-59 (1948).

[7] I. Chein, "Some Aspects of Research Methodology," an unpublished paper.

happy to accept those values which have been evolved through the centuries in man's struggle to define his relationship to his fellow man and which have received their fullest expression in the United Nations Declaration of Human Rights. This value standard is implicit in much of the writing throughout this book, and from it follows our concern with the *reduction* of prejudice. The latter serves as the base line for our evaluative comparisons in following chapters.

Social research is, by its very nature, a cooperative endeavor. Many poeple and agencies have contributed to the present research. Without the generous support of the Marshall Field Foundation neither the present book nor the research upon which it is based would have been possible. We owe a deep debt of gratitude to both the Newark and the New York housing authorities and their staffs for their constructive cooperation throughout the study. Their objectivity and their concern with the broadening of knowledge are in the best traditions of public service and public responsibility.

Dr. Bryn J. Hovde was a valuable guide in the field of interracial housing; his insights and experiences contributed much to our initial orientations. Dr. John S. Harding and Dr. Robert K. Merton were helpful in preliminary planning conferences. Dr. Merton generously made available to us the research experiences of his housing studies which had been supported by the Lavanburg Foundation. Drs. Gordon W. Allport and M. Brewster Smith were kind enough to read an early draft of our manuscript and to make various suggestions.

We are grateful to the many, necessarily anonymous, housing officials throughout the country who gave us the benefit of their experiences and informed judgments about factors affecting interracial relations in public housing projects. We also owe much to the conscientious efforts of interviewers and coders; some of the latter, particularly Lydia Deutsch and Ruth Evans, worked long and late as volunteers.

Most of all, we are indebted to our colleagues at the Research Center for Human Relations. Dr. Marie Jahoda has contributed ideas and suggestions throughout the research; many of her suggestions are incorporated into the text. Dr. Stuart W. Cook, the director of the Research Center for Human Relations, has been a constant guide and source of stimulating suggestions. He has made many valuable contributions to all phases of the research. He has helped with its planning, with its execution, and with its writing. Few authors are indebted more than we to him.

Not the least of our indebtedness is to Miss Sally Cohen and Mr. Norman Miller for their secretarial assistance in bringing this book to completion.

Morton Deutsch
Mary E. Collins

Research Center for Human Relations
New York University
June 1950

Interracial Housing

CHAPTER I

The Significance of Interracial Housing

SHELTER is an essential of all human existence. This fact has long been recognized but only in recent years have the American people accepted as their public responsibility the provision of decent housing for those in need.

Public housing in the United States has, as part of its comparatively short history, an emergency character. The federal housing program under the Public Works Administration in the thirties was sold to the public and to congressional committees on the grounds not only that the program would provide better homes for more people, but also that the construction of the houses would provide work for the unemployed. Later, the emergency need for shelter for war workers provided the impetus for more building of public housing units. Currently, public housing and publicly assisted housing is being used as a partial answer to the serious housing shortage and to the need for slum clearance and urban redevelopment. In the *Housing Act of 1949* Congress declared that: ". . . the general welfare and security of the Nation and the health and living standards of its people require housing production and related community development sufficient to remedy the serious housing shortage, the elimination of substandard and other inadequate housing through the clearance of slums and blighted areas, and the realization as soon as feasible of the goal of a decent home and a suitable living environment for every American family, thus contributing to the development and redevelopment of communities and to the advancement of the growth, wealth, and security of the Nation. . . ." [1]

This declaration of national housing policy provides American cities with a unique opportunity. Almost every city in the United States has one or more blighted areas — blocks of dreary tenements and

[1] From Section 2 of the *Housing Act of 1949* (Public Law 171, 81st Congress).

shacks in run-down industrial areas. These slums are the breeding place of crime and delinquency; they are the source of broken families, tuberculosis, fires, and truancy. They consume public services such as police and fire protection much more extravagantly than other areas but return far less in taxes. Pretty much anything that is bad can be found in these deteriorated neighborhoods. The *Housing Act of 1949* brings the opportunity to clear away many of these slums.

But it does more than give a chance to clean up bad neighborhoods. Its broader significance is that the public housing and urban redevelopment programs will inevitably help to shape interracial relations in the United States for many years to come. This is true because deteriorated districts are usually the locales to which Negroes, Chinese, Mexicans, Puerto Ricans, and other minority groups are confined by practices of residential segregation.

We have two alternatives as we enter a period of rapid expansion in public housing and as we prepare to destroy our slums. We can either house people according to their needs without regard to their race, religion, or national origin, or we can create, much as we have done in the past, segregated communities "For Negroes Only" or "For Whites Only." There is at present much controversy concerning the alternative to follow.

The argument of those opposing segregation is that if we choose the latter course (since this is housing being built with the assistance of public funds), segregation is, in effect, being given an *official* stamp of approval. The origin of this stamp, they point out, is not likely to go unnoticed by people throughout the world as they listen to American statesmen plead the cause of democracy, nor is it likely to have little effect upon the inhabitants of neighborhoods so stamped. Further, they indicate that if we choose the path of segregation in public housing and in urban redevelopment, we shall actually do much to promote the rigid separation of racial and ethnic groups in many areas where a sharp separation does not exist. The large-scale nature of public housing developments, the unified administration of projects, and the homogeneity of policy frequently mean that if a segregated policy is implemented large numbers of dwelling units are either assigned to "white" or "Negro" tenants. There is, thus, little opportunity for the natural interplay of many social and economic factors to cause a racially mixed neighborhood. The administrative decision, since it covers large residential neighborhoods, serves as a rigid barrier preventing the natural breakdown of segregation in some areas.

The proponents of segregation, on the other hand, state that Ne-

groes and whites do not mix, that "trouble" results when Negroes
and whites live next to one another, or simply that a policy of nonsegregation will not work. They assert that there is no sense in trying
to force people who do not want to live together to do so, and they
stress the notion that Negroes, as well as whites, want to live with
their own kind. As support for their position, they cite the once re-
vered sociological doctrine that "stateways cannot change folkways."

These, then, are some of the conflicting viewpoints with respect to
residential segregation. In subsequent chapters, we shall present evidence which is directly relevant to these opposing viewpoints but,
below, let us briefly consider the significance of residential segregation.

THE IMPACT OF RESIDENTIAL SEGREGATION

There are many reasons why residential segregation can be considered to be of central importance to intergroup relations in general.
First of all, residential segregation brings with it, as a natural consequence, segregation in many other areas of living. If Negro and
white people do not live near each other, ". . . they cannot — even
if they otherwise would — associate with each other in the many
activities founded on common neighborhood." [2] Segregated racial
neighborhoods tend to bring with them segregated schools, recreational centers, shopping districts, playgrounds, theaters, hospitals,
leisure-time facilities, etc. Thus, one result of residential segregation
is that prejudiced whites have little opportunity to see Negroes in
social contexts which bring out the fundamental *condition humaine*
of Negroes and whites. They do not see the Negroes, for example,
as school children disliking homework, as expectant mothers in their
first pregnancy, as tenants complaining about their landlords, or as
breadwinners facing a contracting labor market. Moreover, the latent
hostility in the segregated, exaggerated by the guilt feelings of the
segregators, is likely to result in behavior which will provide a further rationale for prejudice and segregation. Residential segregation
has a dynamic which tends to be self-perpetuating and reinforcing of
prejudice.

Residential segregation, in yet another way, is of central importance. Next to employment discrimination, segregation is probably
the most significant way by which Negroes, as a group, are disad-
vantaged.[3] Residential segregation for Negroes in the North has always resulted in increased competition for a limited number of dwell-

[2] G. Myrdal, *The American Dilemma* (Harper, 1944).
[3] R. Weaver, *The Negro Ghetto* (Harcourt, 1948).

ing units, with the consequence that Negroes have invariably paid higher rentals for poorer accommodations. With limited incomes, high rentals have resulted in severe over-crowding and rapid physical deterioration. The economic and psychological burdens resulting from these housing conditions have contributed notably to a high incidence of delinquency, broken homes, emotional instability, and to the general brutalization of life. These characteristics of Negro ghettos also tend to support the rationales for prejudice, helping to perpetuate the vicious circle which Myrdal and others have fully documented.

THE POTENTIAL SIGNIFICANCE OF RESEARCH ON INTERRACIAL HOUSING

Public housing has existed for more than ten years. It has had a chance to develop standard patterns and variations with respect to racial occupancy. The common pattern is complete segregation — Negroes and whites live in separate housing projects — but there are important exceptions. These exceptions and the variations among them, in effect, provide a natural social experiment which permits those engaged in carefully controlled social research to gather valuable information about the conditions which make for wholesome race relations. Such research can, by providing scientifically grounded knowledge in the place of current uncertainties, aid policy makers in their efforts to live up to the principles of the democratic ethos in their official functioning.

The moral pressures of the American Creed are relatively difficult to evade in official governmental actions. This is not to say that there are not strong pressures from realtors and others to run counter to this creed in public housing policy. Typically, official policy makers are placed in conflict with respect to the issue of segregation in public or semipublic housing developments. Frequently they make no decision, letting chance circumstances determine occupancy policy; or they may decide in favor of segregation and justify their position by saying that "Negroes and whites don't get along together," or that mixing them will cause "trouble." It is precisely because policy makers have such conflicts and evade decisions that research in this area can be of strategic social usefulness.

Not only may such research be socially useful (by facilitating social change in a direction which would decrease the discrepancy between social ideals and social reality) but it might also have theoretical significance. Most of the studies of attempts to change prejudice have, by and large, been limited to influences which were relatively minor in relation to other influences in the subject's social milieu. It seems probable, however, that a major social innovation such as the creation of publicly supported interracial housing communities is likely to influence strongly the social milieu of the residents in such communities. It has long been recognized that the home and its environs are very important transmitters and determiners of social attitudes.

Thus, social distance scales provide support for the belief that neighborly contacts are of the more intimate types of contact. Whites who assert that they would have no objections to having Negroes attend the same school, work alongside them, or go to the same church with them may still reject the idea of having Negroes as neighbors. This being so, there is reason to believe that the housing community, in addition to being a particularly strategic point of focus in the efforts to develop more wholesome interracial relations, is a fruitful setting to test and develop theory. It, perhaps, provides one of the few opportunities for interracial contact of a sufficiently intimate and extended nature to result in large attitudinal change. In light of the crudity of most attitude measurement techniques, changes of relatively large magnitude are necessary to make possible identification and measurement of significant theoretical relationships.

It is for the reasons outlined above that we came to feel research on interracial public housing would be of significance. To orient ourselves to the field of interracial housing, to obtain the insight of people with experience in this area, and to determine the social urgencies and the vital issues, we interviewed housing officials throughout the country. The information and orientation obtained in the course of this survey is presented in the next chapter. While we are unable to provide answers to many of the issues which are presented there, we feel that the outlining of the basic problems and points for decision may be of value in stimulating research and in sensitizing interested people to the factors which may influence interracial relations in public housing.

The remainder of the book reports research bearing on a central issue in interracial public housing, the question of the racial occupancy pattern: "Shall we assign families to dwelling units within a project without regard to their race, creed, or national origin? Or shall we, for example, assign Negro and white families to separate areas or separate buildings?" We have selected for investigation, through controlled research, housing projects which follow each of these alternative principles. Our interest was in studying the effects of these different types of projects upon their tenants. We have been concerned with the implications of the decision about the occupancy pattern for the behavior, the attitudes, and the social relations of the housewives and children, Negro and white, who live in the projects. Our findings have relevance, we believe, to current controversies in the press, in the courts, and in Congress about segregation. They throw light on the socio-psychological implications of the "separate but equal" doctrine which appears to be the last line of defense for those who are reluctant to face the future.

A Survey of the Experience of Housing Officials

THEIR VIEWS ON FACTORS INFLUENCING INTERRACIAL RELATIONS[1]

Social scientists are not by profession housing experts. While the former can and should bring psychologically and sociologically relevant questions to any specific social situation, nevertheless, practitioners in housing know from experience where difficulties exist, what methods seem to be the best, what is realistic, and what is idealistic. It was to such practitioners experienced in the administration and managing of interracial housing projects that we went for opinions on factors influencing intergroup relations in interracial public housing. Personal interviews with forty-two housing officials in the eastern, midwestern and far-western United States produced the complex and challenging picture we shall report in the following pages.[2] From this compilation of experience and delineation of problems crucial to practitioners we hope to define socially useful and scientifically meaningful problems for research.

Our discussion of intergroup relations with practitioners in the field of housing centered around three groups of persons: The first are those responsible for the formulation of plans and policies, those who select sites, sign contracts, set personnel policies, and make public statements. These persons are in federal and local housing agencies. We shall call them the *Policy Makers*. The second group of persons referred to are those whose task it is to carry out over-all policy in

[1] The study upon which this chapter is based was conducted by Mrs. Collins.

[2] Informants included race relations advisers in the Office of the Administrator of the Housing and Home Finance Agency, national representatives of the Federal Housing Administration and the Public Housing Administration, present and former executive directors of housing authorities, former national and area personnel of the Project Services Section of the Federal Public Housing Authority, public housing managers, and persons currently engaged in research in housing.

the day-to-day business of running a project and to administer policy within the framework set by the Policy Makers. We shall call these persons the *Management*. And, finally, there are the *Tenants* themselves. The influences of these three groups on the total picture of intergroup relations are obviously interrelated. However, for purposes of reporting, the data collected may be grouped meaningfully under these three headings.

THE INFLUENCE OF POLICY MAKERS

Policies are set in various ways: some as the result of discussion and reflection, some as the result of pressure from interest groups, many on the spur of the moment or as the result of a specific event. Our informants recounted experiences with all species of policy decision. The comment of one informant highlighted what is perhaps the basic consideration: "The all-important thing is that the question of racial occupancy and all questions attached to it should not be answered by accident. The tenants themselves tend to be ignored in favor of such considerations as expense, patronage, or esthetics by the planners, but the question of potential occupancy by different racial groups must not be overlooked and every aspect of the planning must be considered from a long-range point of view. How will this affect the housing market? Shall we have a bi-racial or an integrated project and what does this mean in terms of expense for dual facilities? Will we have a recruitment problem if we place the project here? All of these questions must be brought up at the planning table; they are not incidental questions but basic ones."

The policy decisions which are most critical in intergroup relations in an interracial housing project, according to the experience of our informants, are those related to site selection, project and neighborhood facilities, management selection, quotas, occupancy pattern, public relations, and consistency of policy.

Site selection. It was stated emphatically by several of the informants that interracial housing projects should be located in interracial neighborhoods. To support this view the following reasons were offered:

1. In order to comply with legislation which provides that public housing be equally available to all racial groups, it is essentially "dishonest" to locate a new project where one or the other groups will have either physical or psychological difficulties to overcome in order to move into a new neighborhood.

2. Fringe areas which meet both the requirements of both slum clearance and interracial composition are easily found in any city.

3. Most housing authorities have neither the interest nor the wherewithal to promote an educational program among civic leaders, neighborhood leaders, or potential project residents to convince them that large shifts of one group or the other to a previously homogeneous neighborhood can be realistically accomplished without opposition, tension, and "trouble."

4. The difficulty of recruiting and retaining the white group when it feels itself to be in the minority must be realistically appraised. It was observed that a neighborhood typically tends to become more Negro rather than more white. As a consequence, it is difficult to maintain a constant ratio of one group to the other after the Negro population has become the majority in any given area.[3]

The implication here is that it is unrealistic to expect either white persons to move into a "Negro neighborhood" or white families to remain in a neighborhood which is predominantly Negro. One informant said that the ideal neighborhood for an interracial housing project would be an interracial neighborhood which is predominantly white.

5. The effect on intergroup relations of locating the project in an interracial neighborhood is to provide an easy adjustment for project residents from both ethnic groups. In an interracial neighborhood neither group feels isolated at the outset, and certain neighborhood facilities may be present which are usually not available immediately either to the Negro or to the white group in a new neighborhood, e.g., barbers, hairdressers, bowling alleys, movie theaters, banks, restaurants, and churches. It was also pointed out that the schools in an interracial neighborhood are usually interracial; this lessens the burden for either Negro or white children in adjusting to the new environment.

The choice of an "open site" equidistant from the centers of concentration of both racial groups, it was suggested, may result in the avoidance of many site selection problems. While it may be difficult to convince persons interested in the slum clearance aspect of a public housing program of the desirability of starting afresh with a new community, it was suggested by some informants that from the long-range point of view of many city planners, the remaking of an old congested neighborhood is not an auspicious method of site selection.

A compromise between the interracial neighborhood and the open site was recommended by one informant: "I would say, after saying that it's hard to pick a site and that the wrong site can defeat an announced interracial policy, that for the minority group (Negroes)

[3] A full exposition of this phenomenon is found in Gunnar Myrdal's *An American Dilemma* (Harper, 1945).

a "fringe" neighborhood is the best. However, all things considered, I think that if a site can be found that is not too far distant from an *interracial* neighborhood, that an interracial project might best be situated in an all-white neighborhood."

Two informants raised the question of policy on tenant selection procedures in connection with the question of site selection. They pointed out that if tenants are selected from a city-wide pool of applicants, if an effort is made to keep all eligible persons in the community in a current file, and if prospective tenants are given opportunities to move into vacant units on the basis of need and the date of their application, then the racial composition of the neighborhood surrounding the site of the project tends to have less effect on the composition of the tenant population. Where tenant selection is done separately for each project and the initiative to place applications in more than one place is left up to the resident, then, they said, the influence of the project site has its maximum effect.

Project and neighborhood facilities. A housing project is a new community. Often the density of population for the area is considerably increased. To what extent should the housing authority concern itself with questions of play space, washing machines, drying areas, parking space, storage space, and club rooms? To what extent is it the housing officials' business to concern themselves with adequate transportation, shopping, educational, and recreational facilities in the project neighborhood? And do differences in the quality and quantity of facilities affect intergroup relations within the project?

The majority of the informants felt very strongly about the possible effects of project and neighborhood facilities on intergroup relations. One informant stated: "You can't expect decent human relations unless you have a decent community." Another said: "This is a community job too, not only the job of the housing authority, though it's up to the housing authority to see that it's done. When a community like a project is set up, it's going to stand for 150 years or more — that's why it's important to plan for the 'trims'; we don't want glorified slums. How many housing projects do you suppose are put up without conferences between the Housing Authority and the Department of Education, the Department of Parks, or even the Department of Sanitation? Everything a new community needs should be thought of and then something should be done about it. When one housing project was put up in ———, the authority just assumed that retailers would recognize business opportunities and would set up grocery stores and meat markets. What did mushroom up in the area were second-hand furniture stores. The tenants were mad at everybody."

Another informant said: "Inadequate facilities both in and out of the project mean bad feeling and conflict. And it is so easy to take it out on the opposite group. I think that the adequacy of community facilities determines the potential of community cohesiveness; and, conversely, the fewer the facilities, the less cohesive the groups; and the more asocial people become, the more they look out for themselves."

Several of the informants observed, in partial contrast to the above, that grievances about facilities may, and sometimes do, result in tenant organization and cooperative action to correct these inadequacies. Many examples were cited, such as tenants organizing a cooperative store, a buying club, or car pools and setting up their own nursery schools or kindergartens. As one informant put it, "The answer, of course, to inadequate facilities is good neighborliness."

The consensus here is that the provision of adequate in-project facilities and the planning for out-project facilities in cooperation with other city agencies and outside organizations is one of the responsibilities of the planners and policy makers. All of the informants, however, stated that one must be wary of the concept that the provision of facilities, especially recreational facilities, is a panacea for hostile intergroup relations. Adequate facilities may be a necessary but not a sufficient condition for the high tenant morale and noncompetitiveness which may be considered prerequisites for good human relations. Inadequate facilities may have either of two different effects. They may cause, on the one hand, low tenant morale, general griping and discontent, and competition between tenants — all conditions which may easily lead to "scapegoating," competition between groups, and disproportionate use of available facilities by one group. On the other hand, inadequate facilities may bring about the cooperative action of residents to change conditions for the total group, the result of which may actually be improved intergroup relations. Research to determine the circumstances which will lead to cooperative rather than to competitive action in the face of adversity would be of considerable value.

Management selection. All of the informants agreed that it is desirable to have housing authority and management personnel from different ethnic backgrounds. However, the importance attached to an interracial staff differed markedly among the informants.

A spokesman for one group stated: "Never, never try to operate

an interracial project with a segregated staff. By happenstance, up-
grading and turnover and the like, you can wind up with a racially
homogeneous staff. This should not be allowed to happen even if it
means promotions out of turn. If your staff realizes the job in human
relations which is being attempted and has confidence in your sincerity, job assignments made out of normal order can be explained
and the explanation accepted." The reasons given by these informants
for an interracial staff at the project level are these: Negro and white
interviewers, receptionists, and other office personnel demonstrate
clearly that the project is being run by both groups and for both
groups, that management is acting in the manner that tenants are
being asked to act, and that the status of all groups in the project is
equal. An integrated pattern in the project offices carries the prestige
and sanction which will help to make this the socially accepted pattern in the housing community.[4]

Policy makers in housing authorities, the informants emphasized,
must take responsibility for the selection of management staffs who,
in attitude and behavior, will be wholeheartedly behind a policy of
encouraging good human relations in housing projects. Interracial
staff composition by itself is not enough, they assert, since over-
concern with maintaining an interracial staff can result in a token
minority group representation, "window dressing" as it was termed.
The real concern must be with the behavior toward tenants of every
staff member from the executive director to the janitors. In the words
of one informant: "If an authority has committed itself to an interracial housing program and appoints an executive director who dis-
agrees with this part of the policy or who even thinks it might be
a mistake, the chances for the program being a success are pretty slim.
Sure, top management must be qualified in many other ways but attitude toward this aspect of the program is basic. Especially at the
beginning, there are countless decisions which the director and his
managers have to make and questions to be answered which have important consequences in terms of the success of an interracial program. Unfortunately, once a project has been opened up to all persons who are eligible it isn't enough just to hope that everything is
going to take care of itself."

It was pointed out that if the authority sees its job in terms of
providing shelter only, the implications for job descriptions and staff

[4] The comparable recommendation that Negro personnel being brought into a previously segregated industrial plant be introduced first in the office branch has been
made by several writers. J. A. Davies, *How Management Can Integrate Negroes in
War Industries*, is the source of one such recommendation (Albany, N.Y., State War
Council, Committee on Discrimination in Employment, 1942. 43 p.).

organization are different than if the authority assumes additional responsibility for promoting tenant welfare. If the former concept prevails great emphasis will be placed on having a manager with real estate and business experience and the staff will be limited to persons selected for their ability to maintain the project, lease the apartments, collect the rent, and balance the books. If, however, public housing is seen as "more than bricks and mortar," staff personnel must possess human relations skills as well as the technical skills needed for the management of real estate. Moreover, such a concept may require that the staff be augmented. Additional staff members may include: (1) housing assistants whose job it is to establish and maintain contact with tenants, (2) an administrative assistant whose function it is to release the manager from details which prevent him from establishing contact with tenants and with outside public service agencies, and (3) a community coordinator or project services person to act as liaison between project and agencies, to promote tenant activities, and to handle or refer tenant problems. At the authority office level, additional staff might include advisers or coordinators for the functions listed above, a research staff for the periodic appraisal of different aspects of the program, and a race relations consultant.[5]

Quotas. The seriousness and urgency of the question of setting quotas was demonstrated by the fact that the issue was repeatedly brought up in spite of the fact that it was not mentioned in any question. A decision to set limits on the number of Negro persons admitted to a project involves a choice between two social values which have high priority in the value systems of the persons who were interviewed: (1) the desire to see the development of harmonious intergroup relations, the chances of which, it was asserted, are significantly reduced when the percentage of Negroes in a project goes much above the 50 percent mark; and (2) the desire to see no discrimination for whatever reason operating in our society. As one informant voiced the dilemma: "I hate to answer this question. I even hate to think about it. I used to think I knew the answer. Now I have nightmares. In the first place, this is the most crucial question facing public housing, but the answer isn't in housing alone. The percentage of Negroes in a project *shouldn't* go over what it is in the community at large,

[5] There is considerable disagreement among housing officials as to whether a race relations consultant, as such, is advisable or necessary. It is the considered opinion of several of the informants that on the local authority level race relations is everybody's job, that there are no problems which are race problems unless they are created by the authority itself, that the problems which do arise between different groups are human relations problems which everyone on the project staff should recognize as such and be able to handle as such.

everything else being equal. The catch, of course, is that everything else isn't equal. The problem is that when you have a project where the percentage of Negroes is as high as say 80 percent, you just don't have an integrated project. With everything frozen for Negroes, in time an interracial project can become a Negro project. The only solution, of course, is more housing and a more mobile Negro group. Now I can't honestly state a case for quotas, yet from the point of view of intergroup relations it unfortunately makes sense." [6]

One informant stated emphatically that this dilemma was more apparent than real and felt he could demonstrate that income level could be used as the criterion for eligibility without this leading to segregated, all-Negro housing. The statistical data on income levels and substandard housing required to debate this point are outside the scope of this report. The pertinent fact here is that all of the persons interviewed felt that given conditions as they are today — the housing shortage, the relatively lower income of the Negro group, the disproportionately less housing available to the Negro group, and the reluctance of the white group to remain in an area where they begin to feel in the minority — the question of quotas, not for the purpose of keeping Negroes out of a project, but rather to prevent a project from becoming all Negro, does present an important policy problem.

Occupancy patterns. All of the informants agreed that the integrated occupancy pattern is to be preferred. A few informants added, ". . . if you can do it." The following reasons were offered for this recommendation: (1) It makes for ease in operating the project, including the optimal use of space and facilities; (2) it is morally "right"; (3) it has the most beneficial effects on the attitudes of residents toward members of different groups.

(1) It makes for ease in operating the project. The managers who had had experience in integrated projects said simply that they personally would hesitate to undertake the management of a bi-racial project because of the problems created: dual facilities, lack of flexibility in the assignment of dwelling units, and what would amount to the management of essentially two separate projects. In addition to these reasons, the added expense of operating a bi-racial project was cited: "If you're really going to have equal facilities in a partially segregated project, for example, you have to plan for two of everything. But not only do expenses go up when you start talking dual facilities, but more time and therefore more money goes into keeping

[6] Charles Abrams, in "The Segregation Threat in Housing," *Commentary,* Feb. 1949, presents the arguments for considering quotas as the means to inclusion of minority groups rather than as a means to exclude them.

everything straight when it comes to assignments of dwellings, re-tenanting empty apartments and the like. Also, rent money is often lost when a unit becomes vacant and it must remain vacant until just the right shade of skin color comes in to apply for it."

(2) It is morally "right" to have integrated projects. Several in-formants began their remarks with a statement to the effect that no matter what decision was made at the policy level regarding the oc-cupancy pattern and for whatever reasons — expediency or public pressure or lack of courage — any pattern save an integrated one was a compromise with basic democratic ideals. As one informant put it, "Segregation is an all or none affair. You either segregate or you don't. Buildings, areas, or projects, it's all the same and you have the same problems both administrative and human." Another informant said, "Even with a checkerboard pattern[7] you have ghettos — meaning everything that that word implies."

The comment of one informant, successful at selling both the local housing authority and the community on a policy of integration, is pertinent here: "I used to preach equality, rights, democracy, the works! But I don't any more, not that I feel it less strongly. Adminis-trative arguments are much more formidable and I simply take the offensive and ask, 'How would you run a segregated project?' That's quite a question and the management problems it raises are innumer-able. I must say I never had anyone answer that question either to my satisfaction or his."

(3) The integrated occupancy pattern has the most beneficial ef-fects on the attitudes of residents toward members of different groups. All informants felt that the ultimate effects of the integrated occu-pancy pattern were improved intergroup relations between persons living in the project. The informants were not agreed on the question of whether the effects of a bi-racial occupancy pattern on intergroup relations were, in the long run, beneficial or harmful. Some stated that, although the bi-racial project raised problems, its effects on the interracial attitudes of tenants might be better than if they were liv-ing in all-white or all-Negro projects. Another group stated the opin-ion that segregation on the same site was worse for intergroup rela-tions than segregation in the community. The reasons given for this position were these: Day-to-day experience with barriers erected by a group in authority accentuates differences, sharpens cleavages, and fosters rivalries; differences sharply focused by proximity to the other group tends to increase the feelings of superiority of the majority

[7] Separate buildings for Negro and white tenants, but with the buildings inter-mingled.

group and the feelings of inferiority of the minority group;[8] and attempts to encourage members of the different groups to participate in activities together, as is sometimes done, or to share facilities can justifiably evoke the tenant response of, "Why should we? We're different, aren't we? The fact that we're separated proves it."

Public relations. Three aspects of public relations as it relates to the interracial policy of the local housing authority and to intergroup relations in the project are (1) general announcements to the community at large about the housing program, (2) announcements of the intended interracial policy designed to reach the market of potential residents from all groups, and (3) announcements to prospective tenants at the time of signing the lease. About one third of the informants felt that these questions were not of much moment. In their opinion, the critical housing shortage means that every person within a radius of fifty miles knows when one brick is placed atop another during the construction of a project and promptly makes moves to apply for occupancy. However, approximately two thirds of the informants felt that perhaps not enough thought was given to the possible effects of the lack of a public relations policy. The opinions of the latter will be discussed in the three categories mentioned above.

1. General announcements of policy to the community at large. Many housing officials are worried about the detrimental effects of an unenthusiastic community and unenthusiastic tenants on the future of public housing. One of the ways to build support for a public program is to disseminate information which emphasizes the positive aspects of the program. Such material may or may not include information about the interracial policy of the authority.

Differences in the manner of public presentation of the authority program is immediately apparent in the examination of annual reports. In some reports, emphasis is placed on the statistical data concerning the costs, the number of persons housed, the rate of turnover, and the construction details. In other reports, in addition to the foregoing, facts about the project residents are included. In these latter reports, not only is the matter of race brought up, but it is given considerable prominence; in addition, a "selling job" on the idea of public housing is done. These reports highlight such information as the areas in the community in need of redevelopment, the correlaries

---

[8] The point made here is in effect the consensus among social scientists as reported in a study by M. Deutscher and I. Chein, "The Psychological Effects of Segregation: A Survey of Social Science Opinion," *Journal of Psychology*, 1948, 26: 259–87.

of substandard housing as exemplified in tuberculosis rates for the different sections of the city, and the socially useful job the authority is accomplishing in raising the standard of living of its many tenants.[9]

2. Announcements of interracial policy to potential residents. It is generally agreed that the fact that an interracial housing project is going to be open to other than white persons does "get around." However, the way in which this information "gets around" was felt to be extremely important by many of the informants. The main reasons given for making announcements about eligibility for occupancy were these:

a. Rumors about public housing projects are known to be fantastic. Rumors that only persons on relief are eligible, that this project is only for Negroes, that the next project is going to be for whites, that the lights are put out at ten o'clock, that incomes are checked weekly, and that no one is allowed to have overnight guests are examples of the sort of information which may be picked up in the neighborhood of a project under construction. One corrective for this, of course, is to make available authoritative facts to the contrary.

b. Because minority group members are unused to assuming that an addition to the community, whether it be a housing project or a swimming pool, is going to be open to them, it is necessary to make quite clear that all persons meeting stated requirements are eligible for occupancy. This is especially important, it was felt, at the beginning of a given housing authority's program. All of the informants were agreed that an announcement on interracial policy should be clear, positive, and factual and should not preach. It was suggested that, in addition to an unambiguous announcement, certain indirect informational devices such as the following could be employed: running newspaper pictures of prospective tenants of all ethnic groups in line for applications; pictures of the interracial project staff; pictures of the playground of another project, from another city if need be, showing Negro, oriental, and white children playing together. The informants felt that early knowledge of conditions for occupancy makes for a less hesitant and less anxious group of applicants for housing. The possibility that a clear announcement results in a selection

---

[9] Judging from the content of a series of debates among housing officials at a public housing conference meeting, a very real concern among housers is the question of the relative weight which should be placed upon the negative social conditions which make a public housing program necessary and the positive results of a slum-clearance program. The question is whether or not a member of a Congressional Banking and Finance Committee is more likely to be moved to appropriations by the argument that people will be happier, better citizens in a decent dwelling place or by the public accusation that babies in his district are being bitten by rats.

among white tenants to include the less bigoted was considered quite likely.

3. Announcements to prospective tenants at the time of leasing. Once a person has been declared eligible for an apartment in a housing project, he is given the opportunity to agree to certain conditions, to sign a lease, and to move into a new home. At this point, an opportunity arises to restate the authority's interracial policy. Opinion differed as to whether the opportunity should be used. Some informants felt that by the time tenants reached the interviewing stage, they knew about the policy and that to bring it up only provoked unnecessary discussion. Others held that interracial tenancy is a matter which is of concern to a prospective tenant and it is "fair" to give him an opportunity to discuss it. It is a matter he himself may hesitate to bring up. The time of leasing, when a tenant is accepting other conditions, making other agreements, and asking other questions, is the ideal time to make quite certain that he understands and accepts the fact that his next-door neighbor may differ from him in racial background. In the words of one informant, "It's terribly important to make explanations beforehand. We told our tenants, 'If you sign this lease, you'll be entering an interracial neighborhood; it will be interesting; you'll be part of a great American experiment!' In other words, a willingness to accept this situation and cooperate was made a condition of the lease." All of the informants who favored making an announcement felt that it should be done in a personal, friendly way. They recommended statements which clearly implied that objections or opposition would result in no change of policy, yet at the same time assumed that tenants could consider living in an interracial project desirable.

Consistency of policy. All of the informants agreed that a consistent, definite policy toward eligibility, selection, and placement of tenants favored the development of good intergroup relations. Supporting reasons given were: the elimination of uncertainty for persons executing the policy was necessary for a good management job; uncertainty built up expectations among prospective tenants which were in line with their preferences and therefore raised questions about and bred opposition to the interracial policy; and where there was vacillation in policy, pressure might more readily be brought to change it.

Here it was pointed out, however, that if the authority was just beginning its program, it might be well to evade the discussion of plans for an interracial occupancy pattern until the time for applications, at which time the community would be presented with a *fait accompli.* This practice, it was said, avoided the possibility of opposition crystallizing into formidable pressure on the authority. But, it was added, once the policy was announced, it should be definite and unswerving. Some of the informants said in this connection that accusations of being secretive, bureaucratic, and autocratic were often leveled at authorities which took the stand that eligibility would be determined by need only, regardless of the race of the applicant. Persons making this accusation take the position that the questions of what groups will occupy a public housing project should be referred to the community. However, it was the consensus among the informants that eligibility for housing on the grounds of race should not be a matter for debate and that given the social climate in most communities, the result of a community referendum would be segregation of racial groups.

Several informants pointed out also that, especially if an authority is tenanting integrated projects, individual and group opposition should be anticipated and steps to meet such opposition should be developed. Such steps might include soliciting support from outside community groups known to favor interracial housing. The majority of the informants recounted personal experiences where, in the face of a threatening group, political party leader, or individual tenant, they had simply said, in effect, "No, this is the way things are." Whereupon, they reported, effective opposition usually disintegrated. The point was also made that when one makes a concession or indulges in any favoritism, in connection with race relations complaints (or, for that matter, on other questions) one's reputation for fairness, an essential ingredient of an administrator's reputation, is lost. In this connection, it was observed that the gossip level in projects is extraordinarily high and that very little management activity passes unnoticed.

THE INFLUENCE OF MANAGEMENT

"Management," for present purposes, includes the executive director of the authority and his central office staff, the project manager and his staff, and the superintendent of the buildings and his staff — that is, any person who represents the authority in any capacity. It is the task of these persons to carry out the day-to-day business of running the projects within the policy set by the policy makers; theirs is the responsibility for such things as setting practices, making decisions, answering questions. The influences of these people on the attitudes and behavior of the tenants they serve will be discussed under these headings: management's intergroup behavior and attitudes, handling tenant problems, and promoting tenant activities.

Management's intergroup behavior and attitudes. The emphasis placed by all of the informants on the concepts that good intergroup relations in the project was part of doing a good job and that "race relations" was not a special skill relates discussions here to statements made in the previous section. The discussion on the effects of management's attitudes covered essentially these points: (1) the impact and importance of management's behavior toward all of the tenants, (2) the jobs on the project of greatest potential influence on intergroup attitudes, and (3) the need for training of the management staff.

All informants agreed that management sets standards of behavior in the project and that the impact which management can have on the intergroup relations is very great. One informant said, "For most people living next door to a white person or a Negro person, as the case may be, is a new experience. Even if he agrees to it, he doesn't know how he's supposed to feel about it for sure.

"Tenants will try you out if you give them the chance. If one of them can get by with little remarks like 'this place is swell if it wasn't for the ——s all over,' he'll know that he isn't supposed to like it. But if you call him on a remark like that in a nice casual way and say something about how most residents don't notice any more that there are ——s in the project and hasn't Mr. So-and-so done a nice job on his window box — the guy'll most likely agree. And he'll think twice before he pipes up again. But, on the other hand, if someone in management makes a remark, say a white cashier says to a white tenant as he comes up in line to pay the rent, 'These Negroes are sure slow, we ought to have a separate line for them,' or if a janitor remarks about how much more work tenants who are not members of his own ethnic group make — this is a hint to the tenants about how 'management' feels. Much of that can undo a lot of good intentions."

In answering the question about the effect of staff attitudes, several informants brought up the point that certain jobs in the project were especially important to intergroup relations. These were identified as those jobs where the employee of the authority meets the tenants: managers, interviewers, lease handlers, receptionists, switchboard operators, project service persons, and maintenance people. These persons, it was said, represent the authority for the individual tenant. And, it was contended by the majority of the informants, such employees need some guidance or training at the beginning in how to act.

One woman, the manager of an integrated project, told this story about herself when she was stressing the need for helping new people in the field of interracial housing: "I started here in the authority in the very early days and my first job was helping in a mad rush to get applicants assigned to units for the move-in day. Someway, I got left with the job and all I can say is that I was doing what I thought was right. Anyway, I sorted the Negro and white applications and worked on a fair selection of buildings and started fitting families into the units — Negroes at one end and whites on the other. I was working along and Mr. ———, the executive director, came in and looked over what I was doing. He noticed in an instant that I was working from two piles and he just looked at me and said kindly, 'Why are you doing it this way?' I guess I learned more about race relations in that afternoon than I have any time before or since." Another informant remarked, "Favorable attitudes aren't enough.[10] In fact, favorable attitudes can be a great detriment. You have to know how to act."

While the training of the management staff to handle interracial questions was discussed, no enumeration of the number of training sessions or periodic reviews of problems having to do with the question of human relations or intergroup relations was made. The impression received was that the number is extremely low. One such training session is reported in the housing literature[11] and in the estimation of the individuals responsible for it, it was extremely successful. However, its effects on subsequent intergroup attitudes and behavior of the tenant population were not evaluated in any systematic way.

Handling tenant problems. All of the informants who discussed this question agreed that the management of the public housing project has some responsibility for the general well-being of the tenants. While all felt that management should not usurp the function of a social agency, they agreed it should serve as a reliable source of information for persons seeking advice or assistance. One informant recalled that when public housing first started it was common practice for management to do casework which, in many instances, the housing personnel were neither equipped for nor had the time to do. This was soon recognized as being detrimental both to tenants and to tenant-management relations. However, several informants stated that management should provide a person whose duties include consulting with tenants and suggesting sources of aid.

[10] The term "favorable attitudes" used in the question was commented upon by several of the informants. It was occasionally interpreted to mean the patronizing, lenient, "professional do-gooder" attitude with which apparently a great many persons in housing are unfortunately familiar. We, of course, intended "favorable attitude" to mean "without prejudice" rather than patronizing.

[11] Langdon W. Post, "Race Relations Training Improves Management Job," *Journal of Housing*, June 1947, 4:175–77.

Several informants pointed out the contribution which a representative of management can make to harmonious human relations when talking with tenants about complaints and problems. Difficulties which have a background of interracial prejudice may be reinterpreted for the tenants by such a person.

The relationship of the project management to the social agencies in the surrounding neighborhood was commented upon by all of the informants. It was suggested that this relationship was certainly one criterion of good management. Where the agency is found acting as referee or intermediary in tenant-management disputes, it was asserted, the fault usually lies with the housing management.

In connection with the discussion on this point, the question of the practices of outside agencies which sponsor tenant activities was brought up. According to several informants, an agency whose policy regarding treatment of interracial clientele differs from that of the housing management can have a detrimental effect on intergroup attitudes in the project. One informant stated as an example, "If you are trying to break down barriers between your racial groups and the only agency in town which can help you set up, for example, a well-baby clinic, operates on a segregated basis, you should locate the clinic across the street rather than on the project site. This may or may not change the policy of the agency, but the management's position is strengthened by such a stand." Also mentioned at this point was the fact that management, in cooperation with the social agencies in the neighborhood, can help in the process of integration of tenants into the larger surrounding community.

Promoting tenant activities.[12] The number and variety of tenant activities in any given project depends upon many factors, not the least of which, in the opinion of the informants, is the attitude of management toward such activities. If, as is sometimes the case, management considers organized tenant activities a nuisance, it is relatively easy to discourage them by such devices as keeping community rooms locked, never being available for discussion of plans, or, as was reported in one case, charging money for the use of community rooms. On the other hand, management may encourage or actually promote tenant activities.

The observations and recommendations of the informants who discussed management's role in the encouragement of tenant activities are presented here:

[12] The memoranda, handbooks, and reports, published and unpublished, written by the staff of the Project Services section of the Federal Public Housing Authority cover in great detail the philosophy, methods, job descriptions of personnel, and criteria for evaluation of tenant activities in a public housing project.

1. Management staffs are in a position to make official or semiofficial contacts and arrangements with other city departments, e.g., the Department of Parks and the Board of Education, for personnel and facilities for community activity. They are also in a position to make contacts in order to encourage affiliation of tenant groups with existing interracial groups outside the project. This last was noted as one indirect way of initiating interracial activity, especially of a social nature.

2. Management is in the position to request from the housing authority or to recommend to the authority the provision of space, facilities, or personnel to fill community activity needs.

3. Tenant activity should be tenant initiated and tenant managed but management approved and management aided, most informants agreed. It was observed by several informants that the type of activity is not as crucial in determining intergroup attitudes and behavior as the process by which it is begun and maintained. The "brotherhood" theme or the tone of the professional "do-gooder" was mentioned as something to be avoided. "Most people abhor being uplifted" was the statement of one informant.

4. Any activity which is management approved, aided, or sponsored should be interracial in an interracial project. No groups should be allowed management facilities or receive management cooperation which are organized in such a way as to exclude participation by members of any other racial group.

5. Several informants strongly recommended that the hours of management personnel be staggered and that persons responsible for community activities, if the staff includes such persons, be on the project site during the hours when the tenants have the most leisure time, i.e., evenings and weekends. The periods of greatest tenant activity are observed to be (a) early afternoon, women's free or "freer" time; (b) late afternoon and early evening, children's heavy activity period; (c) early evening and late evening, adult men and women's activity time; and (d) weekends, when men and children have the most free time. In direct contrast to this, it was observed, most management personnel leave their projects at five in the afternoon and do not work weekends.

6. Management, in an effort to promote group activities, should spot and select tenant leaders, it was asserted. One informant said, "No matter how good management is, tenants know their interests and their needs better than the people in the office. If there were some way to do it, it would be best for intergroup relations in a project to select 95 percent of the tenants on the basis of need and the other 5

percent on the basis of leadership ability. There's no way to estimate what a few tenants with the encouragement of management can do to set the tone of a project."

7. Discussion of tenant activities included comments about tenants' councils. As with other tenant activities, management can do much to make or break a tenants' council. A few of the informants stated that where no tenant council exists, management has failed in one of its tasks. They felt that absence of an active tenants' council, partially responsible for community activities, was a sure indication of management's fear of the tenants and of management's general patronizing attitude toward the project.

One informant stated, "Active tenants' organizations should exist but it seems to me kind of naive to assume that persons will come to a tenants' association meeting (a) when there is no emergency, (b) where no special interest groups are in existence, and (c) where management gives the tenants no responsibilities. Where management sincerely feels that a functioning group of tenant representatives is an asset to the project, you will generally find such a group. Sometimes it takes nurturing and some 'manufacturing of problems' for tenant voice and handling, but the ultimate usefulness to management and the resulting heightening of morale among all of the tenant body far outweighs any time and energy management spends with such a group. Of course, it all depends on what management is like; whether management really gives a hoot about the tenants."

There are no housing projects without some group activity. Even if adult groups are limited to occasional gab fests in yards or on benches, the children in the project are active in groups of their own creation. It was the consensus of the informants not only that participation in some group leisure-time activities was desirable from the point of view of harmonious intergroup relations, but also that the existence of some group activity provides the opportunity for the beginning of the neighborliness which characterizes the project where there are harmonious intergroup relations.

Several informants had had extensive practical experience with tenant activities. A summary of their observations and recommendations follows:

1. The number of persons who participate in community activities may or may not be an indication of "good" tenant morale or harmonious intergroup relations. A low percentage of participants or a small number of activities may reflect well-established customs of the community, the leisure-time habits of particular economic groups,

the limitation on activity imposed by particular working shifts, and activities by tenants outside the project.

2. Activities for special interest groups have the best chance for success and the greatest effect on intergroup attitudes. Examples given here were choral groups, athletic teams, committees for special events, and workshop groups. In contrast to special interest groups, such activities as a project-wide dance or street party where tenants get together once for a special activity would have little long-range effect.

3. Short-lived special interest groups were recommended for obtaining the maximum amount of participation. Short-lived committees for a special purpose, for example, may involve persons whose time is limited or who hesitate to commit themselves to any long-drawn-out objective. Tasks accomplished by such committees bring quick rewards; the rewards obtained are based on cooperative effort. The short life expectancy of the committee discourages rivalry for long-range leadership.

4. Small recreational groups which require a small amount of space and do not encourage large numbers of nonparticipant spectators were also recommended. The effect is to have a maximum amount of participation with a minimum amount of self-conscious behavior resulting from observation by on-lookers. This, it was stated, is especially important during the early life of the project.

5. It was indicated that activity which minimizes the necessity for verbal facility lessens the probability of the shy or less well-schooled persons dropping out in the early stages. Until persons "know" one another, they may be very reluctant to speak up or voice opinions in public. Many Negroes, it was reported, are extremely reluctant to speak up in a new interracial situation.

6. Adult activities of the classroom type have little chance for either attracting or maintaining attendance, it was stated. The exception mentioned was adult citizenship classes for the specific goal of obtaining citizenship status.

7. Special attention was called to adolescents and unmarried adults in connection with the discussion of tenant activities. Several informants stated that in an interracial project one always can observe a segregated racial pattern with young unmarried adults, even where there is a great amount of fraternization between children and married adults of the different racial groups. Many informants observed that while provision is made for space and facilities for young children and for adults, e.g., playgrounds and meeting rooms, special out-

door areas are not usually set aside for adolescent use. Similarly, provision is seldom made for indoor activities for young adults. One informant pointed out that an activity such as managing the project library was eminently suited to this age group, since it provided for boy-girl relationships in an atmosphere free of the usual social taboos.

8. No special comment was made on the younger children's activities except for several statements that "the kids are no problem" as far as intergroup relations are concerned. It was pointed out that the children provide the opportunity for parents to meet. Sometimes these meetings do not occur under the best of circumstances. Nevertheless, it was felt that where project conditions called for the co-operative endeavor of parents, no better excuse could be found for asking adults to work together. A fathers' group to fix up a play room and a mothers' group to take turns supervising the children were given as two examples of an activity which is easy to initiate, which satisfies needs, and where acquaintanceships must be made.

9. The central role played by women in the projects was pointed out. Several informants said, "The women run the projects; men may sometimes be the spokesmen but the women run the show." Exámples given were of women-initiated complaints about facilities and regulations and of women cooperating to "better" a specific project condition. One informant stated that in his opinion "The women are the more active in organized groups," and, he added, "It's good too, because I'm sure that women are more prejudiced than men when they move in. The men, who are out all day and tired when they come home at night, tend to be indifferent about many of the project features, but you don't find an indifferent woman very often."

10. The existence of a tenants' council, as has been reported, was felt by a few of the informants to be a measure of project success. Other informants felt that where you have another kind of all-project participation in some tenant-initiated activity, a tenants' council might well be superfluous. The examples given of substitute activity were a tenant-managed cooperative store or farmers' market. Many informants stated explicitly that a high level of good intergroup relations could not be achieved without tenant leadership. In support of this was offered the generalization that any policy planning or activity with any group of persons, to be fully accepted, must be initiated or at least accepted and approved by the tenants themselves.

THE TENANTS

All informants were asked specific questions on characteristics of the tenant population which might be expected to influence the na-

ture of intergroup relations in interracial housing projects. Specifically, questions were asked on the effects of pre-project interracial
experience of tenants and of current interracial experiences outside
the project, the effects of more than one non-white group in the tenant population, the effects of different ratios of white to non-white
tenants, the effects of different religious groups in the project, and the
effects of the temporary or permanent nature of the housing development.

None of the housing officials were able to give definitive answers
or concise observations on any of the above variables. Their intimate
knowledge and experience had been gained most often at the level of
policy and administration, and their criteria for good policy and good
administration tended to be in terms of the gross reactions of tenants
as a group and the efficient running of the over-all project. That
these variables do operate, however, was conceded in every case. How
they operate or to what extent they interact with other determinants
of intergroup relations the officials were reluctant to say.

For example, in discussing past experience one informant said: "I
must give you an academic answer. I'd say that where there's no
previous experience you get more prejudice. In fact, I have a kind of
theory that the farther away people are from an interracial set-up,
the worse they think it is." Another informant said, "There's no doubt
that past experience will make a difference in how people feel about
living next door to a white person or a Negro person. It would be silly
to ignore the possibility that a war worker from Atlanta will find
the ways of a person from Cleveland peculiar in this matter of race.
But, while the individual manager should know something about the
background of his tenants, he should be mighty careful about how
much allowance he makes for it. He should set his standards for his
project, then, if he knows that he's dealing with some people for whom
this adjustment is going to be a little rough, he will just know it's
going to take him a little longer to get the kind of project he wants.
A knowledge of what his tenants are used to or what they expect
should never make a manager lower his standards."

CHAPTER III

The Research Problem: THE OCCUPANCY PATTERN

THE REASONS FOR SELECTING THE OCCUPANCY PATTERN

WITH a census of problems and issues in the field of interracial housing before us, our task was to select a problem for more definitive research. Many studies were suggested by our survey: the effects of different policy decisions, the effects of different management procedures, the effects of different kinds of tenant activities. All of these and many more would be useful. From these possibilities, we selected for study the impact of different occupancy patterns: *the integrated interracial* pattern (families are assigned to apartments without consideration of race) and the *segregated bi-racial* pattern (Negro and white families live in the same project but are assigned to different buildings or to different parts of the project).

We make no claim that the occupancy pattern is the only important influence on racial relations in projects that house both white and Negro families. Quite on the contrary, our survey indicated that the state of racial relations in a project would be affected by many factors of a diversified nature: the neighborhood in which the project is located, the racial composition of the tenants, the attitudes of the management staff, project facilities, etc. The effects of the occupancy pattern would, of necessity, be colored by the influence of these other factors. Thus, a manager in a segregated bi-racial development who is an ardent proponent of interracial amity might stimulate interracial tenant activities and a social atmosphere the effects of which might, perhaps, run counter to the influences of the occupancy pattern.

Yet our decision to investigate the effects of the occupancy pattern, as our first systematic study in this area, was not a matter of whim. We had several reasons for the choice. From our survey of housing officials and from our theoretical expectations, some of which

30

will be stated later in this chapter, it was apparent that the occupancy pattern would very probably prove to be one of the most crucial influences on race relations in housing projects. We had reason to believe that it, perhaps more than any other single factor, establishes the framework which serves to define the social meanings and the social limits of racial relations.

It is not often that social research executed without the instigation of an administrator will be useful in affecting administrative decisions. Nevertheless, a further important reason for our interest in the occupancy pattern is our belief that, under the present circumstances, *something can be done about it* and that research can offer guidance in the doing. Unlike many of the factors which affect the state of race relations in a housing project, the occupancy pattern is directly determined by an administrative decision, a decision which is responsive primarily to the "social climate" rather than to economic and physical limitations. The decisions about occupancy patterns, now that the Federal Housing Program is under way, are about to be made; there is good reason to believe that it is easier to consider than to reconsider such policy decisions. With the political atmosphere such as it is, with the alternative occupancy policies each having their pros and cons with respect to political feasibility, these decisions are particularly apt to be influenced by knowledge of the consequences of the different patterns for tenant relations.

SOME PRELIMINARY ASSUMPTIONS TO GUIDE RESEARCH

Our statement of the problem in the foregoing paragraphs needed much additional formulation before it could serve as a guide to research. In effect, we had to develop hypotheses about the possible effects of the occupancy pattern from our knowledge of the essential differences between the two types of project we were studying and from a knowledge of basic socio-psychological principles. Otherwise research efforts would be dissipated on the investigation of factors not likely to be related to the occupancy pattern.

The essential differences between the segregated bi-racial and the integrated interracial occupancy patterns. In the development of hypotheses, it is always simpler to deal with imaginary, idealized phenomena rather than with events as they occur in the real world. So, for the sake of convenience, let us conjure up two projects exactly alike except for their occupancy pattern. In one project, Negro and white families are assigned to apartments without consideration of race; in the other project, though Negro and white families live in the same project, they are assigned to different buildings or to different parts of the project. It is important to note that in both cases the project is a distinctive entity which doesn't merge into the surrounding neighborhoods either physically or administratively.

From the point of view of race relations, what then are the essential differences between the two projects? The answer to this question depends largely upon circular reasoning; that is, one believes the differences to be essential if the hypotheses that one predicates from these differences allow one to predict important differential consequences between the two projects which can be verified. For reasons which will become more evident as we proceed, it seems to us that the two types of projects differ mainly with respect to (1) the physical and functional proximity of Negro and white families, (2) the social norms regarding racial relations implicit in the policy decision of the occupancy pattern by an official public authority, and (3) the relationship of the project to the broader community.

These are the differences, but what are their effects? The answer to this question requires a further specification of interest. Effects upon what? Our original interest directs us to inquire about the effects of the occupancy pattern upon (1) social relations across racial lines, (2) the social standards for behavior with people of the other race, (3) the general pattern of social relations in the project, and (4) interracial attitudes.

Once some questions for research have been raised, it is not an uncommon procedure for the social scientist to skip on to a discussion of the research procedure and research results proper. To us, however, there seem to be clear advantages in an explicit statement of the main hypotheses and the assumptions which underlie them. By so doing, one places the research in a broader framework of knowledge and can thereby evaluate its consistency in terms of this broader framework. A finding is more trustworthy and more meaningful if it dovetails with other knowledge than if it stands by itself.

A Statement of the Basic Hypotheses for Research

Hypotheses related to the effects of proximity. A fairly well-known principle in psychology of particular interest to us here is the "interaction hypothesis." We may state a special form of this hypothesis as follows: Other things being equal, *the amount of contact between any two persons will increase as the distance between their place of residence decreases.* It is obvious, for example, that a person living in Kalamazoo is more likely to meet another Kalamazoo resident than he is to meet a person located in California. This hypothesis has received a number of interesting confirmations. Thus, it has been shown

that relatively more marriages take place between people whose pre-
marital residences are close than between people whose residences are
widely separated. Friendships in a college dormitory are more likely
to be established with students who room near by.

It is clear that taking the knowledge of the relative physical proximity of Negro and white families in the two types of projects in conjunction with the interaction hypothesis, we can predict that (1)
*there will be more frequent contacts between Negro and white fami-
lies in the integrated interracial than in the segregated bi-racial project.* That is, there is more likelihood that Negroes and whites will
meet and get to know each other in the integrated project. In addition, knowing that Negro and white families in the integrated project
will be in the same buildings as neighbors, sharing many things in
common — hallways, elevators, noisy children, incinerators, basement
facilities, quarrelsome neighbors, etc. — we can also predict a greater
intimacy of contact between Negro and white families in the integrated project. It logically follows, if the preceding is true, that intimate contacts would also occur more frequently in the integrated
project.

One may very well at this point raise a question that is crucial to
interracial housing: Suppose Negroes and whites just don't mix. Suppose, as some of our southern statesmen assume, there is a natural
antagonism between members of the two races if they are in close
contact. What then? If this assumption is true, one would expect increasing hostility with closer contact and one might even then expect
the hostility to function so as to reduce the interracial contact. Under
such conditions, one could not expect the results predicted in the
preceding paragraph.

Let us make the assumption that no inherent antagonism exists
between the two races, that under conditions of equal-status, neighborly contacts the white tenants will find that the behavior of Negroes will be such as not to conform with the stereotypes and rationales which support prejudice. They will find that their Negro neighbors will be no dirtier, no louder, no more drunken, no more aggres-
sive, no lazier, and no less trustworthy than their fellow white tenants.
If this assumption is correct, one would expect not only more frequent
and more intimate contacts in the integrated projects but also more
friendly personal relations between Negro and white families in the
integrated than in the segregated project. This corollary follows
directly from our first hypothesis and from our assumption about the
characteristics of Negro and white people as neighbors. Its truth or
falsity provides a crucial test of the two opposing assumptions about

the relations to be expected between Negro and whites in a situation of close equal-status contact over an extended period of time.

This is not to deny that a prejudiced white person may express hostility and resistance toward entering into or remaining in a situation of close, equal-status contact with Negroes. One may very well expect such a person to show more resistance to moving into the integrated than into the segregated project. However, if he does move into the integrated project and if he stays long enough (as a result, perhaps, of his otherwise unsatisfiable need for housing), our hypothesis assumes he is more likely to have the experiences which will result in friendly relations with Negroes than if he moves into the segregated bi-racial project. The very existence of an integrated interracial project over a period of time without its becoming uniracial or without its being plagued by racial strife is a strong indication that the assumption of inevitable racial antagonism is false.

Hypotheses related to official policy and social norms. It has long been recognized that people tend to behave the way they are expected to behave. The expectations of others in a social situation, particularly if these others are important to the individual, help to define what is the appropriate behavior in a situation. In large measure, the process of socialization of the child consists of his learning to anticipate how people expect him to behave in certain situations and how they will react to his behavior. Knowing the expectations of others and anticipating certain reactions, the child is able to guide his behavior so as to win approval rather than disapproval from his parents or from other adults upon whom he is dependent. In a similar way, the adult in a highly interdependent society is dependent upon the social approval of various people and various social groups. He guides his behavior so as to conform with what is considered to be socially appropriate or desirable behavior; or, in other words, so as to conform with the behavior that is expected in a given situation by the people or groups whose approval is important to him.

In line with this we might expect that the policies of an official, public agency will help to establish social expectations which directly influence behavior. This is, of course, particularly true of an agency such as a Public Housing Authority which controls, for the residents in the public housing projects, the means of satisfying an important need — i.e., the need for decent housing at a low rental. If our expectation is correct, one would forecast that the very existence of and adherence to an official public policy of one sort rather than another with respect to the occupancy pattern would affect the state of race

relations in a housing project. Implicitly, such a policy suggests a social norm for interracial behavior in the housing project; it establishes
expectations as to how one should behave so as to meet with public
approval.

It is not difficult to see how the integrated occupancy pattern might
convey an implicit public sanction of interracial association of a fairly
intimate nature. The lack of separation, the non-distinguishing of
Negro and white tenants (in a society where Negroes have customarily been segregated) implies that race should not be a criterion for
distinguishing among tenants. In effect, the policy of integration
takes sides; it is an official statement of the equalitarian theme of the
American Creed. In interpreting this lack of distinction between tenants, the residents in such a project might see the policy as stating,
"We believe that all men are created equal and, in this project, all
shall be treated equally without distinction on the basis of race, creed,
or national origin."

It is easy to see, also, how the policy of segregation in a bi-racial
project implies a distinction between Negroes and whites and could
be interpreted by tenants to mean that Negroes and whites should
be kept apart. In the context of the history of race relations in the
United States (of a traditionally inferior social status for Negroes)
this distinction and separation connote that Negroes are inferior to
and not to be associated with by whites. Thus, the social norm for
race relations suggested by segregation is that of avoidance of intimate social relations upon an equal-status basis.

For many communities, of course, even the segregated bi-racial
project stands out in contrast to the general picture of residential
segregation. The social norm of the segregated bi-racial project may
therefore imply somewhat less complete separation than the norm
characterizing the broader community. Such a policy does suggest
approval for some equal-status relationships between Negroes and
whites, if only in their relatively impersonal roles as tenants.

Thus, from the above discussion, it seems clear that we can predict
that (2) *the social norms in the segregated project will be less favorable to friendly interracial relations than the social norms in the integrated interracial project.* We would expect support for this hypothesis to emerge from still another source, namely, the operation of the
widely accepted value of neighborliness. Considering most people's
rather parochial definition of "neighbor," the ancient injunction to
"love thy neighbor as thyself" is more likely to appear relevant to
people living next door than to people living in separated buildings.

Thus, it follows that the injunction is more likely to be applied to members of the other race in the integrated interracial than in the segregated bi-racial project.

Social norms in the project and in the community at large. From the preceding discussion, it is apparent that one should expect the social norms in the integrated project to be considerably more favorable to friendly interracial relations than the social norms in the community-at-large. On the other hand, if the norms of the segregated bi-racial project differ at all in this respect from those of the broader community, one should expect them to be only slightly more favorable.

The fact that a housing project typically exists as a part of a larger community rather than in isolation means that the attitudes toward interracial relations of people outside the project may have effects on the people in the project. This is why the discrepancy between the project and the community in standards for interracial behavior is likely to have special consequences for the tenant in the integrated project. For example, one would expect the white housewife in the integrated project to be faced by more dilemmas — e.g., what to do when she wishes to give a New Year's Eve party and to invite friends from outside the project (some of whom are prejudiced) as well as her friends in the project (some of whom are Negroes). Such problems would, one can expect, by analogy from other similar situations, make the issue of race relations a matter of fairly prominent concern; that is, it is likely to be thought of, talked about, or spontaneously mentioned, etc. We can, therefore, predict that (3) *the salience of the interracial aspects of the project will be greater in the integrated than in the segregated project.*

Much accumulated experience seems to indicate that an issue which is salient to a number of people in common frequently draws these people closer together. The issue provides a source of conversation, a basis of common experience; it calls for increased socializing as a means of providing mutual support for opinions and as a way of working out solutions to the problems which the issue represents. Thus, for example, the typical white housewife in the integrated project facing the problem of how to deal with her prejudiced friends from the outside, knowing that other white housewives have similar problems, is likely to discuss these problems with the others and, in the process, be drawn closer to them. Thus, not only can we expect more friendly relations across racial lines but also that (4) *the relations among the white residents will be more friendly in the integrated than in the segregated bi-racial project.* This is a rather surprising possibility which had not occurred to us as we commenced our research planning.

As we present the analysis of our findings, we shall point out further consequences of the discrepancy between the norms for race relations in the project and in the community at large.

The effects of the occupancy pattern upon attitudes. So far, our reasoning has led us to expect that the integrated occupancy pattern will create more opportunities for close equal-status contact with members of the other race and a social atmosphere more favorable to friendly interracial associations. Much evidence is accumulating to indicate that under favorable conditions such as these, equal-status contacts between Negroes and whites tend to reduce prejudice among whites. Studies in the army,[1] of college students,[2] in industry,[3] and in the merchant marine,[4] all point to the same result. If this is the case, one can expect that, as a result of their experiences in the projects (5) *white tenants in the integrated projects will have less prejudices toward Negroes than their counterparts in segregated bi-racial projects.*

In other words, the differences between the two types of projects which have already been indicated would, we anticipate, result in attitudinal differences between the residents in the two types of projects. We can expect these attitudinal differences to be most directly reflected in attitudes toward the Negro people in the project; they might be generalized somewhat to include Negro people in general; and perhaps they might even extend to other minority groups. Of course, since the latitude of favorable change is greatest for the people who originally were most prejudiced, we would anticipate that they would show relatively the most change in attitudes.

In the segregated bi-racial project, the people who were for the most part unprejudiced to begin with are placed in a situation in which there are strong social pressures to avoid close contact with Negroes; to the extent that these pressures are different from those they are accustomed to, they are likely to become more prejudiced as a result of living in the segregated project. That is, just as a preju-

[1] Information and Education Division, U.S. War Department, "Opinion About Negro Infantry Divisions in White Companies of Seven Divisions," in *Readings in Social Psychology* (Holt, 1947).

[2] F. T. Smith, *An Experiment in Modifying Attitudes Toward the Negro* (Teachers College, 1943). G. W. Allport and B. M. Kramer, "Some Roots of Prejudice," *Journal of Psychology*, 22:9–39.

[3] A. Rose, "Race Relations in a Chicago Industry," an unpublished study (Univ. of Chicago, 1946). B. K. MacKenzie, "The Importance of Contact in Determining of Attitudes Toward Negroes," *Journal of Abnormal and Social Psychology*, 43:417–41 (1948).

[4] I. N. Brophy, "The Luxury of Anti-Negro Prejudice," *Public Opinion Quarterly*, 9:456–66 (1946).

diced person is likely to become less prejudiced as a result of experiencing an environment in which the social norms are against prejudice, so, too, an unprejudiced person is likely to become more prejudiced in an environment which is more prejudiced than the one to which he has been accustomed.

To sum up, we have presented in this chapter what we believe are the essential differences between housing projects with segregated biracial and integrated interracial occupancy patterns. Calling upon existing socio-psychological knowledge and theory, we have attempted to predict the effects of these differences upon (1) social relations across racial lines, (2) the social standards for behavior with respect to the other race, (3) the general pattern of social relations in the project, and (4) interracial attitudes. We have given the thinking behind our hypotheses in some detail because of our feeling that the trustworthiness of a research result in part must be evaluated in terms of its consistency with other existing knowledge. To be sure, if our findings run counter to our hypotheses, our basic assumptions will need a thorough reexamination.

CHAPTER IV

The Research Procedure

IN THE previous chapter, for the purpose of developing hypotheses, we permitted ourselves to construct two imaginary projects which were identical except with respect to the occupancy patterns. The social scientist, unfortunately, rarely finds that reality is as accommodating as imagination. Only in imagination is he able to construct housing projects which ideally suit his research purposes. In reality he must investigate what exists.

In the abstract, the research design called for by the hypotheses is relatively uncomplicated. It simply requires a comparative study of a number of segregated and integrated interracial housing projects which are equated in all relevant respects other than the occupancy pattern. Practically speaking, however, the phrase "equated in all relevant respects" introduces enormous complications and difficulties. As any housing administrator will point out, "No two housing projects are alike."

These difficulties in doing research on the effects of different social practices and policies must be realistically faced. Rarely will any one piece of social research provide definitive answers to a question; confidence in research findings, to repeat our thesis of the preceding chapter, must come from the similarity of findings of related or repeated research. This is no argument against the single research project. To the contrary, despite the difficulties, a carefully considered research investigation can give answers which have a higher probability of being correct than any other known method of answering important social questions.

We designed our study to overcome as many as possible of the difficulties which would otherwise distort our findings. First of all, we carefully selected the segregated and integrated interracial projects we were to study so they were as equivalent as possible in all relevant respects other than the occupancy pattern. Second, we decided not to

39

limit our study to one project of each type; we stretched our funds so as to study two of each kind.[1] And third, in our method of investigation we carefully collected data about factors other than the occupancy pattern, to determine whether our results could be explained in terms of these other factors. We shall describe several aspects of the specific plan for the present study in some detail.

THE SELECTION OF HOUSING PROJECTS TO BE STUDIED

There are only a few cities in the country which have integrated interracial housing projects.[2] We obtained the cooperation of one of them and then obtained the cooperation of a neighboring city which had established a segregated policy in its interracial public housing projects. These two cities, New York (the integrated) and Newark (the segregated), are, of course, both large metropolises with considerable similarity in their racial and ethnic composition. Their proximity and the similarity of their business and industry result in a constant interchange of residents. Residents of both cities live in one and work in the other. Newspapers from New York may be found on the newsstands of Newark; radio and television stations originating in either city reach the populations of both. As a result inhabitants of the two cities are subject to essentially similar cultural influences.

Perhaps the greatest difference in the housing authorities of the two cities is a difference in size. The housing program in New York demands an administrative set-up which is extremely complex, thereby removing the individual tenant further from the central office than is the case in Newark.

Both authorities adhere to the same over-all regulations laid down by federal authority; both began their programs at approximately the same time. Each periodically changes the assignments of managers from project to project. In all of the projects studied, the manager had had previous experience in one or more other projects. Both administrations include a person or persons in the central office staff whose major responsibility is handling individual tenant problems.

[1] Of course, it would have been desirable to study many more projects of each type, but we had to limit the research to a scope that was feasible with the financial resources at our disposal. This is a limitation which is, unfortunately, characteristic of most research upon significant social problems.

[2] While there are some fifty-odd cities throughout the United States which have integrated interracial public housing projects, in less than ten do such projects contain a proportion of Negro families that is more than 10 percent, but less than 90 percent, of the project population. This information has been obtained from a preliminary listing of "Racial Occupancy Patterns in Active Public Housing Projects" (as of December 31, 1949) prepared by the Racial Relations Branch of the Public Housing Administration.

There were a number of different factors to keep in mind in selecting projects for inclusion in our study: age of project, racial ratio, type of neighborhood, ethnic composition of tenants, ethnic composition of management, building structure, and project size. Most of the projects that we might be interested in were built during the years 1940 and 1941; thus, the age of the project could be easily equated in the projects to be selected for comparative study. The ratio of Negro to white tenants, however, varied considerably from project to project in both cities. The preliminary survey had indicated that the racial ratio was considered to be a vital factor in influencing interracial relations particularly if either whites or Negroes formed a large majority of the tenant population.

We thus decided that *our principal criterion for selecting "matched" projects in the two cities would be that of racial ratio.* Finding that Bakerville[3] in Newark had two Negroes to every white and Sacktown in New York had 70 percent Negroes, we chose these two projects as our first matched pair. Frankville in Newark divided 50-50 in its racial ratio; the Negro-white ratio for Koaltown, in New York, was approximately 40-60.[4] Since the composition of these two projects was the most similar of the remaining possible pairings, they were chosen as the second pair.

Before proceeding with the study, the neighborhoods of each of the projects were inspected and the managers were interviewed to make sure that no marked idiosyncratic factor was operating which might vitiate the comparison to be made. The neighborhoods of the matched projects were found to be strikingly similar: Frankville and Koaltown are located in rather deteriorated Negro neighborhoods with high delinquency rates. Sacktown and Bakerville are also located in predominantly Negro neighborhoods; here the deterioration and delinquency are not so marked. Another similarity among the projects is that all four have both Negro and white employees on the management staff.

[3] Pseudonyms will be used for the projects.
[4] We originally had hoped to study projects in which the number of Negro families represented more than 10 percent but less than 50 percent of the tenant population. We believed that if there were less than 10 percent there might not be enough opportunities for the effects of an integrated policy to reveal itself. On the other hand, if there were more than 50 percent, the white residents might feel themselves to be in the minority — a feeling which might hinder friendly interracial relations. We now have evidence which suggests that the former belief is fallacious; an integrated interracial project that has as few as 3 percent Negroes (as long as this 3 percent represents more than just a few families) is thought of as being interracial by the white tenants. Though we have no clear-cut data on the second assumption, we were surprised to find, in the integrated projects we studied, relatively few indications of a "minority feeling" among the white tenants.

On the other hand, the projects differ in a number of respects. A brief description of each follows:

Bakerville. About fifteen minutes from the center of Newark, Bakerville is situated in an old residential section. Two- and three-story frame houses, built to the street, alternate with garages, retail stores, and small business establishments along the surrounding streets. The neighborhood is interracial. Bakerville covers an area of approximately two city blocks, divided at the two-thirds point by a two-way city street. This thoroughfare separates the Negro section of Bakerville from the white section. The project houses over 600 families in three-story brick buildings with six or nine families in each stairhall (i.e., using the same main entry way and staircase). Between the buildings are lawns or parking areas; in the center of the buildings, on either side, are drying areas for laundry, play space for children, and numerous benches. The larger play space, including a paved area with basketball standards, is in the Negro section. The project office is also situated on the Negro side of the project, a circumstance which requires the white tenants to walk through the Negro side of Bakerville to transact their project business. In addition to the manager of Bakerville, who is white, there is an office staff of two girls, one Negro and one white. The Negro staff member collects the rents, takes complaints, and refers tenants to the manager.

Sacktown. Located on the outskirts of New York, Sacktown resembles Bakerville in appearance. Its three-story brick buildings, housing about 450 families, contrast with the frame houses in the surrounding neighborhood. The residents of the neighborhood are predominantly Negro. Paved areas within the project provide drying space for laundry, play space, and benches. Sacktown has a woman manager with a staff of two office workers. At the time of the study this group included no Negroes. The maintenance staff, however, is interracial.

Frankville. About thirty minutes from the downtown section of Newark, this housing project is located in the center of an overcrowded neighborhood of substandard dwellings, manufacturing plants, taverns, railroad sidings, and junk yards. The project itself consists of three-story brick buildings placed around a large central play space. It houses about 300 families. The buildings for whites are located on one side of the rectangular play court, with parking areas, lawns, benches, and drying areas between the buildings. The Negro side of the project is identical in design to the white. The project office, situated at one end of the court equidistant from either side, is staffed by two persons: the manager, a Negro man, and his assistant, a Negro woman who handles the major part of the day-to-day business with the tenants. The maintenance staff is interracial.

Koaltown, in New York, houses some 1100 families in six-story elevator buildings. The project, however, is in two sections separated by private dwellings and business establishments and a city thoroughfare. The section of the project studied is the larger one of approximately 700 families. Save for the height of the buildings and the absense of outdoor drying areas, Koaltown resembles the other projects in appearance. Paved play space, lawns, and benches separate the brick buildings. The neighborhood immediately surrounding Koaltown is a deteriorated, semiresidential, interracial neighborhood. The dwelling units in the neighborhood are three- and four-story tenements built to the street. These buildings are interspersed with unkempt vacant lots, candy stores, grocery stores, and taverns.

The project office, located in the larger section of the project, has an interracial staff. The manager, a white woman, is aided by a Negro and a white assistant, each of whom is in effect the manager for approximately 500 families. The receptionist and switchboard operator is a Negro girl; the woman who collects the rents is white. The maintenance staff is interracial.

THE METHOD OF INVESTIGATION

From our preliminary survey and the theoretical analysis, it became clear that the focus of the study would be the tenants themselves. Since there was, by and large, little evidence of much organized or observable group activity, it was evident that the main source of our information must come through interviewing.

The interview was long and intensive. On the average, it lasted about an hour and a quarter; some interviews ran over two hours. During the interview data were obtained in five major categories:[5]

1. The attitudes of the housewives toward living in the project. Each housewife was asked what she liked most and least about the project; what her feelings were about public housing, the neighborhood, the apartment, etc.; the anticipations she had before moving into the project; her future plans; and her feeling toward people in general in the project.

2. Attitudes toward Negroes.[6] A series of questions attempted to

[5] The questions asked in the interview are presented in Appendix F. The interview being described here was the one used with white housewives; essentially the same interview, with appropriate modifications, was used with the children and Negro housewives.

[6] Essentially the same questions were asked of the Negro housewives, but, of course, we asked them about white people.

uncover the attitudes of the housewife toward Negroes, her feelings about them, her "knowledge" and beliefs about them, and her feelings about living in the same project with them.

3. The amount and intimacy of contact with other women in the project. Questions were asked about neighborly contacts (such as visiting, shopping together, minding children, going to movies together), friendships, how one gets to know people, etc. Information was obtained about the types of contacts with Negro women.

4. The social supports for attitudes. The housewife was asked, for example, to tell how her relatives, her friends, people in the project, the management staff, etc., would react to her being friendly with Negro people.

5. The characteristics of the housewife. A comprehensive list of questions was asked about the housewife — her age, number of children, her activities, her education, her religion, her interests, etc. — to obtain information about the comparability of the populations in the projects we were studying.

The interview, for the most part, encouraged the respondent to answer freely in her own words rather than to restrict her answer to "Yes" or "No." It took place in the respondent's apartment.

THE TENANTS TO BE INTERVIEWED

Because of the limited number of interviews that our resources made possible, it seemed advisable to concentrate on some segment of the tenant population. We decided to collect our data primarily from white housewives. We made this choice mainly on the ground that the home is largely the domain of the woman. She spends more time in it than anyone else; she is, by and large, the initiator of activities and contacts that develop directly out of the home. Whether or not she "wears the pants in the family," she is the key person in activities centered in the place of residence.

It was not financially feasible to interview both Negro and white housewives in equal proportion. We decided to interview more white housewives as a result of our conviction that prejudiced interracial attitudes are more socially crucial among whites than among Negroes. Segregation and discrimination are, after all, enforced by the white, and not by the Negro segment of the population.

All in all, we interviewed approximately 100 white and 25 Negro housewives in each of the four projects.[7] In addition, 24 Negro and

[7] More exactly, we interviewed 102 white and 24 Negro housewives in Koaltown, 90 white and 25 Negro housewives in Sacktown, 100 white and 24 Negro housewives in Bakerville, and 101 white and 26 Negro housewives in Frankville.

white adolescent boys and girls were interviewed in a project in each of the two cities. The interviewees were selected by a random procedure.[8]

The problem of the comparability of populations in the two types of projects. Underlying the research design and the interpretation to be made of the research results, there is a basic assumption which should be stated explicitly: *The differences which may be discovered with respect to interracial contacts and attitudes between the people in the two types of projects reflect differences in their experiences while living in their respective projects.*[9] That is, we have endeavored to plan the study in such a way that the differences we are reporting cannot be explained by factors other than the difference in the occupancy pattern — for example, by differences between the tenants in the two types of projects in interracial experiences and attitudes prior to moving into their projects.[10] We, unfortunately, have little direct evidence on this last point; attitudinal studies were not made of the tenants as they moved in.[11]

A priori, there seem to be two major reasons to suspect that our assumption of equivalence of attitude among the tenants entering the different types of projects may be invalid: (1) The very fact that New York has an integrated policy and Newark a segregated policy may reflect basic differences in interracial attitudes in the populations of the two cities. New York residents may be less prejudiced than Newark residents; this may also hold true for the residents in the public housing projects in the two cities. (2) Even if the former does not hold, one might expect selective factors to operate unless checked by stronger forces. We would expect the highly prejudiced individual not to move into an integrated interracial project unless he were des-

[8] For a discussion of the method of selecting interviewees and of training the interviewers see Appendixes C and D.

[9] Although the discussion is primarily directed to the comparability of white tenants in the two types of projects, another assumption we are making is that the Negro tenants are also essentially similar. We are assuming that, for example, the Negro people in the Newark projects did not conform to the commonly held stereotypes, any more or any less, than the Negro people in the New York projects. There is little reason to expect differential selectivity by Negroes in tenanting the two types of projects. Information about the characteristics of the Negro population in the two cities as well as our interviews with the white housewives in all four projects provides indirect support for this assumption. See Chapter VIII.

[10] Our interviews with the managers of the various projects, our inspection of the neighborhoods, and the examination of other available data about the projects preliminary to our study had the purpose of ruling out projects if they were markedly different in ways other than the occupancy pattern. Much relevant data did not exist; prior to our interviewing of tenants, we could obtain little reliable data about the tenants — their education, religion, political attitudes, etc.

[11] For a discussion of some indirect evidence see Appendix B.

perately in need of housing; such an individual might have less objection to living in a segregated bi-racial project.

However, certain considerations which are relevant to the question of selectivity at the time of tenanting may be mentioned at this point.

1. The housing need in low-income groups, even during the thirties, was desperate and has grown more, rather than less, intense since then. To be eligible for admission into a public housing project, the need had to be particularly desperate, since only a small percentage of those in need could be admitted. The accommodations offered in public housing projects are incomparably superior to those generally available for low-income groups. The consequence was that the rate of refusals was very low — estimated as less than 5 percent in both authorities. Refusals were, of course, based upon many reasons, only a few of which are relevant to race. Voluntary move-outs during the existence of the projects under study were also very infrequent.

2. The apparent freedom of choice with respect to interracial housing is somewhat different for applicants in New York and Newark. In New York, at the time of tenanting of the integrated projects under study, a prospective resident could only move into an integrated project. No segregated projects existed and no vacancies existed in the few older all-white projects. All other available projects were integrated; none were segregated bi-racial. To avoid living in an integrated project, the prospective tenant in New York would have to continue in his very inadequate housing and ignore the lures of the clean, cheap, and highly attractive apartment in the housing development.

In Newark, the situation was somewhat different — the majority of the public housing projects were all-white, many of them constructed at about the same time as the segregated bi-racial projects. By resisting assignment to the interracial project (if he were able to convince the tenant selection office that, for example, he wanted to live near his crippled mother) the prospective resident might conceivably have gained entrance to a uniracial project. Thus, theoretically, the prospective tenant in Newark had more freedom to be selective than did his counterpart in New York. The net result of such selection, of course, would have been to admit the less prejudiced whites to the segregated bi-racial projects in Newark — an outcome which would reduce the size of the differences our hypotheses call for.

3. The final consideration has to do with the total impression these projects are likely to make on prejudiced whites. All four of the projects are located in predominantly Negro neighborhoods. Even though a prejudiced person can ignore Negro families living in other build-

ings, he cannot escape the pervasive "Negro" impression visually created by the neighborhood. The point is that to a prospective prejudiced tenant in Newark the perception of a segregated bi-racial project will psychologically be very similar to the perception of an integrated project to a prospective prejudiced tenant in New York. Little differential selectivity would, therefore, be expected.

In addition to the foregoing considerations, information collected during the interviewing throws further light on the comparability of the people in the various projects. Of particular interest here are the questions we asked to determine the housewife's previous experiences with Negroes, her education, her religion, and her political attitudes. Lack of comparability on these matters may reflect differences (such as population differences between Newark and New York) other than that due to selectivity; if, however, selectivity was at work during the tenanting of the various projects one would expect it to be reflected in differences among these characteristics of the housewives. That is, it is not unreasonable to assume that if the housewives moving into the New York projects were less prejudiced before their moving, this lesser degree of prejudice would be associated with their previous experiences with Negroes, the amount of their education, their type of political belief, their religion, or some combination of these factors.

From our data, it is clear that the housewives in the two types of projects were not completely comparable on factors, other than the occupancy pattern, which conceivably might influence interracial contact and attitudes. This is, of course, much what one would expect and is one of the hazards of doing social research in real-life settings.

Religion, political attitudes, and education are the major sources of differences among the people in the various projects. Table 1 summarizes these differences. Comparing the integrated interracial projects, Koaltown and Sacktown, with their "matched" segregated bi-racial projects, Frankville and Bakerville, it is obvious that there are more Jewish people in the former — the New York projects. In addition, the people in these projects tend to be somewhat more liberal politically than their counterparts in the Newark projects. It is also clear that the women in Sacktown have relatively more education than the women in the other projects.[12] In both Sacktown and Koal-

[12] The proportion of white residents in Sacktown has been increased from about 15 or 20 percent to approximately 30 percent over the last several years at the initiative of the housing authority. As a consequence of veteran's preference, a large percentage of those moving into Sacktown since the war are veterans attending college under the G.I. bill. These veterans and their families are, for the most part, Jewish, politically progressive, comparatively well educated, and relatively unprejudiced. This group represents approximately 19 percent of the people interviewed in Sacktown.

TABLE 1. PERCENTAGES OF HOUSEWIVES IN EACH PROJECT WITH DIFFERENT RELIGIONS, EDUCATIONS, POLITICAL ATTITUDES, AND PREVIOUS EQUAL-STATUS CONTACTS WITH NEGROES

	Integrated Interracial Projects*		Segregated Bi-Racial Projects*	
	Koaltown (102)	Sacktown (90)	Bakerville (100)	Frankville† (101)
Religion				
Protestant	4%	18%	23%	16%
Catholic	19	43	67	40
Jewish	74	32	7	42
Other	3	7	3	2
Education				
Only public school	47	30	51	42
Some high school	28	35	33	36
Completed high school or more	15	34	14	14
Attended school outside U.S.	10	1	2	8
Political attitudes				
Liberal	36	36	18	26
Middle of road	33	25	37	36
Conservative	31	39	45	38
Previous contact with Negroes				
(1) As friends				
Has had Negro friends	18	29	30	19
Has not had Negro friends	82	71	70	81
(2) As fellow workers				
Has worked with Negroes	26	36	33	33
Has not worked with Negroes	74	64	67	67
(3) As residents in same block				
Has lived on same block with Negroes	16	20	22	33
Has not lived on same block with Negroes	84	80	78	67

* "Koaltown" and "Sacktown" are pseudonyms for the two integrated interracial projects; "Bakerville" and "Frankville" are pseudonyms for the two segregated bi-racial projects.

† The figures in parentheses indicate the number of cases on which the percentage figures are usually based. There are slight variations in the number of cases from table to table because of no responses, unclear answers, omitted questions, etc.

town, religion, education, and political attitudes are highly interrelated. The people with liberal political attitudes are most likely to be Jewish and relatively well educated and the people with most education are also most likely to be Jewish. This is not to assert the converse — that most of the Jewish people in the projects are liberal or relatively well educated. On the contrary, only a minority are politically liberal and only a small percentage have completed high school.

A priori, it is extremely difficult to tell how important the differences in religion, education, and political attitudes are in relation to prejudice. Several studies have found relationships between prejudice and these factors. If these relationships hold for our subjects, one would expect the New York tenants to have been somewhat less prejudiced before moving into their projects than were the Newark tenants. Or, if these relationships did not hold at the time the tenants moved in, we should consider the possibility that these factors (religion, education, and political attitudes) predispose one to become less prejudiced under circumstances such as prevail in either of the types of the occupancy pattern we studied. In any case, *it is clear that in the analysis and presentation of our results, it will be necessary to eliminate or control the effects of these population differences in order to attribute causal significance to the effects of the occupancy pattern.* In subsequent chapters we shall present considerable evidence to show that the effects of the occupancy pattern upon intergroup attitudes are in fact of considerable strength in comparison to the relationships between these attitudes and such factors as education, religion, and political attitudes.

Before proceeding, however, it is relevant to indicate that the white housewives in the "matched" projects are rather similar in terms of the amount of intimate, equal-status experiences they have had with Negro people prior to living in the project.[13] (See Table 1.) Knowledge of the differences in previous experiences with Negroes would not by itself, of course, lead one to expect that the women in the New York projects were, before living in the projects, either more or less prejudiced than their counterparts in Newark. Nor does the absence of such differences prove that the housewives in the two types of projects were similar in their original attitudes toward Negroes. Nevertheless, it is reassuring, because a number of studies have indicated that the amount of equal-status contacts with Negroes is more closely related to the degree of prejudice than are the more indirect, sociological characteristics we have discussed above.

[13] This is true also when patterns of previous experiences are considered.

CHAPTER V

Getting to Know People of the Other Race

As OUR knowledge about the development of prejudice has increased, it has become more and more evident that prejudice rarely originates in personal experiences with the members of a minority group. An interesting investigation conducted by Bogardus[1] a number of years ago provides an apt illustration: He measured the prejudice of students toward various ethnic groups — Germans, English, Turks, etc. The results showed that the students had great prejudice toward the Turks. Few of them, if they had their way, would wish to engage in any type of social relation with a Turk. Yet most of them had never seen a Turk and had no personal experiences which could account for their attitudes. Similarly we know that many people who are intensely prejudiced against Negroes or Jews have never known a Negro or a Jew.

If prejudice is rarely formed as a consequence of personal experience, how then does it develop? Murphy and Likert have given us an answer: "The individual usually acquires his prejudices against a minority group not primarily from contact with this minority group, but chiefly from contact with the prevailing attitude toward this minority group."[2]

Prejudice is, thus, largely acquired through contagion. The tone of voice, the choice of words of the narrow-minded mother or teacher, the cartoons in the comic book, the jokes of the comedian, the villains in the movies and the pulp magazines, the sensational rape and murder stories in the newspapers, the myths and legends circulated by the purblind, and the social practices of segregation and discrimination which imply invidious distinctions — all these are infecting agents. Of course, some people are more susceptible to infection than

[1] E. S. Bogardus, *Immigration and Race Attitudes* (Heath, 1928).
[2] G. Murphy and R. Likert, *Public Opinion and the Individual* (Harper, 1938).

are others. The studies of Adorno, Frenkel-Brunswik, *et al.*[3] have given us an insight into the types of personality that are most subject to contamination by bigotry. However, it would be misleading, indeed, to think of prejudice as primarily reflecting individual maladjustment; healthy as well as neurotic individuals absorb the prejudices of their social milieu.

Prejudice is primarily a social disorder and, as such, it tends to perpetuate itself by the effects it creates. First of all, prejudice places members of a minority group at a social disadvantage. Members of such a group, as a consequence, may develop certain social and psychological characteristics which, in turn, may function to support prejudice. Thus, Negroes placed at a disadvantage with respect to education, employment, and housing may be uneducated, unambitious, or untidy. Prejudiced whites, ignoring their responsibility for this state of affairs, may use these conditions to justify prejudice.[4]

The social policies which place the members of a minority group at a disadvantage — discrimination, segregation, exclusion, etc. — also limit relationships with minority group members to situations which are impersonal or to situations in which the minority group members have an inferior status. Thus, prejudice results in a reduction of intimate, equal-status contacts with members of the minority group. Thus, the prejudiced white person, because of his prejudices, doesn't get to know Negro people intimately in an equal-status relationship. His prejudices combine with social custom to prevent him from having the types of experiences with Negro people which would destroy his prejudices. Hence, the main source of information about Negroes comes to be the "experiences," beliefs, and feelings of other prejudiced members of his own group. As a consequence, members of the prejudiced group, through contact with each other, tend mutually to confirm and support one another's prejudices. A vicious circle or a "socially shared autism"[5] is established whereby, without personal experience with members of a minority group, contact with the prevailing attitude toward them provides the "experience" to support a prejudice.

[3] T. W. Adorno, E. Frenkel-Brunswik, D. J. Levinson, and R. N. Sanford, *The Authoritarian Personality* (Harper, 1950).

[4] R. K. Merton has coined the very apt phrase, "the self-fulfilling prophecy," to describe such phenomena. See his *Social Theory and Social Structure* (Free Press, 1949).

[5] Gardner Murphy has originated the term "socially shared autism" to refer to phenomena such as these in which a social group develops considerable confidence in their belief about something with which they no longer have contact, as a consequence of the members' reinforcement of each other's beliefs. See his *Personality: A Biosocial Approach to Origins and Structures* (Harper, 1947).

Perhaps the first problem that faces the person who wishes to change the attitudes of a prejudiced individual is that of breaking through this vicious circle so as to bring to bear upon the bigoted the experiences necessary to a change in attitudes. Something must be done to "prevent" the prejudiced person from selectively avoiding the experiences which might disrupt his prejudices. One method of accomplishing this objective would be to "compel" him to get to know Negro people in equal-status contacts of a sufficiently intimate and extended nature to resist perceptual or memorial distortion. This latter qualification must be inserted because we know that attitudes tend to select and distort experiences so as to maintain themselves. However, persistent, intense experiences that are repeated are likely to survive attitudinal distortion, if only because of the individual's need to accept the "reality of his own senses and experiences." [6]

All of this means that the individual's needs, conformity pressures, etc. must be utilized to bring him into situations where he is required to behave in ways which are inconsistent with his attitudes (i.e., into situations which he would selectively avoid if he were guided solely by his prejudiced attitude).[7] There is no doubt that the housing shortage has created an opportunity to establish such a situation. Very few of the white tenants in either the segregated or integrated interracial projects that we have studied would have moved into a project containing Negro families if they were guided solely by their attitudes. Their intense need for housing compelled them to move into a situation which they would otherwise have avoided.

In Chapter III we expressed the hypothesis that the closer physical proximity of Negro and white families in the integrated interracial, as contrasted with the segregated bi-racial, projects would result in more frequent and more intimate contact between them. In other words, the opportunities to get to know members of the other race should be greater in the integrated projects. Let us consult the data.

THE LIKELIHOOD OF GETTING TO KNOW NEGRO PEOPLE IN THE TWO TYPES OF PROJECTS[8]

In the interview we asked the housewife to indicate whether she thought that a person who moved in would "be likely to get to know

[6] It is important to emphasize the strength of the motivation to accept as real one's perception and experiences. If they were not customarily accepted, the individual would be in a continuous state of insecurity and indecision.

[7] See I. Chein, M. Deutsch, H. Hyman, and M. Jahoda (editors), "Consistency and Inconsistency in Intergroup Relations," *Journal of Social Issues*, 5, No. 3:2–61.

[8] Unless otherwise specified, the data we present will be based on the interviews with the white housewives.

any colored people in the project." The differences between responses of the housewives in the two types of projects are striking. More than 95 percent of the women in each of the two integrated projects assert that a person will get to know some Negro people in the project; the few dissenters voice the opinion that it "depends upon you." In contrast, only a minority (30 percent in one and 21 percent in the other)[9] of the housewives in the segregated bi-racial projects feel that there is any chance to get to know Negro people; the majority are quite convinced that no such likelihood exists. One housewife in Bakerville sums up a typical reaction quite aptly in her response, "We're in separate parts. They stay on their side and we stay on our side."

Clearly, then, the opportunity to get to know Negro people is considerably greater in the integrated than in the segregated interracial project. Table 2 helps to explain why there is such a striking differ-

TABLE 2. PERCENTAGES OF HOUSEWIVES INDICATING THEIR MOST LIKELY
CONTACTS WITH NEGRO PEOPLE

Type of Contact	Integrated Interracial Projects		Segregated Bi-Racial Projects	
	Koaltown (102) *	Sacktown (86)	Bakerville (43)	Frankville (42)
As neighbors in the building .	60%	53%	0%	0%
Through laundry facilities located in or near building ..	13	17	0	0
Outside on benches	46	64	7	21
In office, etc.	2	1	7	17
At tenant meetings	2	17	28	28
Shopping in stores, in the streets around project	12	13	81	60
Through the children's schools	1	3	14	0

* The figures in parentheses indicate the number of cases on which the percentage figures are based. Only the people who responded "yes" or "uncertain" to the question of getting to know Negro people are included. The percentages may add up to more than 100 because many people named more than one place.

ence in this respect between the two types of project. The most frequently mentioned places of contact with Negro people for white residents in the integrated projects are the buildings in which they live, through laundry facilities located in or near their buildings, or outside

[9] To avoid burdening the reader, we shall not present statistical tests of differences between the two types of projects. These tests, however, have been made and it can be stated that any difference stressed in the text is statistically significant in the sense that it would not occur more than 5 times out of 100 by chance alone. For a further discussion see Appendix D.

on benches. (People in the projects, for the most part, customarily tend to sit during the warm season on benches located near their buildings.) In contrast, the relatively small percentage of housewives in the segregated bi-racial projects who indicate a likelihood of getting to know Negro people in the project specify as the most likely meeting place the stores outside the project where they do their shopping. Thus, only incidentally does the segregated project provide the occasion for interracial contact; the contacts that do take place occur under rather casual circumstances and are of brief duration.

The interviews with the Negro housewives give similar results. *All* of the Negro housewives in each of the integrated projects assert that a Negro person who moved in would "be likely to get to know some white people in the project"; in contrast, almost two thirds of the Negro housewives in the segregated projects say there is no such likelihood. The contacts mentioned through which a Negro housewife is "most likely to meet white people" are closely similar to those mentioned in the responses of the white housewives in the two types of projects as presented in Table 2. It seems evident that the major source of Negro-white contacts (contacts which arise from living in the same building) is not available to residents of a segregated bi-racial project.

Other data which we have collected also give strong evidence of the importance of proximity as a factor in determining the people whom one gets to know and with whom one tends to make friends. Thus, a housewife has most chance (per available persons) of getting to know and becoming friends with people on her floor. The next most probable locale for acquaintances and friends is in the stairhall, the next most probable is the remainder of the building, etc. Thus, of course, if Negro families are on the same floor, there is a much higher probability of getting to know them than if they are in a separate part of the project.

However, it is interesting to note that friendships and acquaintanceships with Negro people are not limited in the integrated projects to Negroes living in the same building. Sixty percent of the women in Sacktown and 25 percent of the women in Koaltown know some Negro people from other buildings "pretty well"; in contrast only 3 percent of the women in the two segregated projects report knowing any Negro people in the project "pretty well."

Physical proximity is not sufficient by itself to explain the above results. There are a sizable number of apartments in the segregated projects which are physically as close to Negro buildings as are the adjacent buildings in the integrated projects. Clearly, other factors are also at work. Two of them may be (1) the social norms with respect to interracial associations in the project — we have previously hypothesized that in segregated projects "one doesn't associate closely with Negro people"; (2) the tendency of friends and acquaintances to introduce each other to their friends and acquaintances. Making friends and acquaintances of the opposite race within the building will thus tend to result in making more such friends and acquaintances outside the building.

THE INTIMACY OF CONTACT WITH NEGROES

In our earlier discussion of the tenacity of attitudes, of their resistance to disrupting or challenging experiences, we indicated our belief that a deeply ingrained attitude such as prejudice, which constantly receives so many social reinforcements, will be changed only as a result of intensive experiences with which the prejudice cannot be reconciled. A superficial acquaintance with one's Negro neighbors may not be sufficiently intimate to provide such experiences. Little is known about the conditions which promote or hinder the development of close, friendly relationships among neighbors in an apartment house or housing project. Thus, a priori, there is no particular reason to expect that Negro and white people living as next-door neighbors in a housing project are likely to get to know each other with sufficient intimacy to destroy stereotypes.[10] Nevertheless, one would, of course, anticipate more intimacy of social relations between Negroes and whites in the integrated projects.

From our interviews we can provide three measures of intimacy of social relations: (1) getting to know "pretty well"; (2) getting to know "best"; and (3) degree of "neighborly relationship."

Getting to know "pretty well." "Know pretty well" is, of course, a subjective matter. We asked the following question: "Do you usually call the women you know pretty well here in the project by their first or last names?" We followed this with, "How many women do you know 'pretty well'?" As indicated previously, only 3 percent of the housewives in the segregated projects reported knowing any Negro residents "pretty well"; in contrast, 49 percent of the housewives in Koaltown and 77 percent of them in Sacktown have at least this degree of social intimacy with one or more Negro people in the proj-

[10] There is some reason to suspect that in a low-income housing project such as the ones under study, closer neighborly relationships would develop than in a higher income group. The fewer telephones, the smaller amount of funds available for transportation expenses, the fewer automobiles, etc. would all function so as to make the resident in a low-income project more dependent socially upon people who live near by.

ect. The differences between Koaltown and Sacktown are large and require further analysis; comment on the differences will be made in a later section of this chapter.

If the percentage of housewives who say that one would be likely to get to know Negro people is compared with the percentage of those who know at least one Negro person pretty well, the outcome for the two types of projects is markedly different. For Koaltown the ratio is 2 to 1, for Sacktown it is 1.2 to 1, for Bakerville it is 10 to 1, and for Frankville it is 7 to 1. That is, in Koaltown and Sacktown (the integrated projects), where one is more likely to get to know Negro people, a greater proportion of those one gets to know will be known "pretty well." Thus, the integrated projects, it will be observed, result in both a greater *absolute* number of interracial contacts of a certain degree of intimacy and more intimacy in those contacts that do take place.

Getting to know "best." The questions which the housewives were asked included the following: "Will you tell me the five persons in the project you know best?" "Are any of them colored persons? If so, which ones?" The results reveal that *none* of the housewives in the segregated projects include Negro people among those they know best in the project. In contrast, 27 percent of the women in Koaltown and 62 percent of the women in Sacktown indicate that at least one of the women they know "best" is Negro. Similarly, only 3 of the 50 Negro housewives interviewed in the two segregated projects state that at least one of the women they know "best" is white; in the integrated projects, more than half of the Negro women interviewed make this assertion.

The degree of neighborly relationships with Negro women. Some of the crucial differences between the two types of projects, we have suggested, arise out of the fact that neighborly types of contacts are physically more possible in the integrated projects. Merely from living as next-door neighbors in one type of project and not doing this in the other, we would expect that the opportunities to engage in neighborly activities would be vastly different. We have asked questions about the following types of activities: (1) visiting back and forth; (2) helping one another out, for example, with shopping, or with taking care of the children, or when somebody is sick; (3) informal club activities, such as "card" clubs and sewing or ironing clubs; and (4) going out together, like going to the movies, shopping together, or going "downtown" together. We have constructed a crude index of neighborly relationships by counting the number of different

TABLE 3. PERCENTAGES OF WHITE HOUSEWIVES HAVING NEIGHBORLY CONTACTS (VISITING WITH ONE ANOTHER, HELPING ONE ANOTHER, BELONGING TO INFORMAL CLUBS TOGETHER, AND GOING OUT TOGETHER) IN THE PROJECT

Number of Neighborly Contacts	Integrated Interracial Projects		Segregated Bi-Racial Projects	
	Koaltown (102)	Sacktown (89)	Bakerville (100)	Frankville (100)
Neighborly Contacts with Negro Women*				
None	61%	28%	99%	96%
One	18	18	1	3
Two	16	21	0	1
Three	5 〉39	24 〉72	0 〉1	0 〉4
Four	0	9	0	0
Neighborly Contacts with White Women†				
None	6	12	9	12
One	8	17	22	22
Two	25	18	31	26
Three	43 〉94	41 〉88	38 〉91	31 〉88
Four	18	12	0	9

* All of the white housewives who report neighborly contacts with Negro women also report such contacts with white women.

† Some of the white housewives who report neighborly contacts with white women also report such contacts with Negro women. The percentages of such women, those reporting neighborly contacts with both races, are indicated in the top half of the table.

types of activities engaged in. Table 3 presents the number of different types of activity engaged in with Negro women for the different projects.

The differences in Table 3 are clear-cut. They indicate that the white housewives in the integrated projects engage in a much wider range of neighborly relationships with Negro women than do the white housewives in the segregated projects. Only 4 percent of white housewives in Frankville and 1 percent in Bakerville have any type of neighborly contact with Negro women; in contrast, the figures for Koaltown and Sacktown are 39 percent and 72 percent, respectively. Comparing the interviews of the Negro housewives in the two types of projects, we find similar results; 44 of the 50 women in the segregated projects indicate *no* neighborly relations with white women; this is true for only 14 of the 49 Negro women interviewed in the New York projects.

These differences, the second half of Table 3 reveals, are not simply a reflection of the level of neighborly relationships among women in general in the four projects. Thus, 91 percent and 88 percent of the white women in Bakerville and Frankville, respectively, have at least one type of neighborly contact with other white women in the project; in contrast only 1 percent and 4 percent of these same women have any neighborly relationships with Negro tenants. Similarly, if we take the ratios between the two sections of the table for any degree of neighborly relationships for each of the projects, we find that in relation to the prevailing level of neighborly relationships in the projects, the integrated projects have distinctly more neighborly relationships between Negro and white women than do the segregated projects. It is interesting to note in the second half of Table 3 that the levels of neighborly relationships are higher in general in the integrated projects. One may speculate here as to whether the restriction of intraproject relationships with Negroes leads to restriction of relationships with whites as well. This point will receive a more thorough examination in a subsequent chapter.

To sum up, the data we have presented so far have demonstrated that the likelihood of white tenants getting to know Negro people and of having intimate social relationships with them is reported to be considerably less in the segregated than in the integrated projects. It seems clear that this difference is due to the opportunities for Negro-white contacts which arise from living in the same building in projects of the latter type.

THE EFFECTS OF THE OCCUPANCY PATTERN VERSUS THE EFFECTS OF RELIGION, EDUCATION, AND POLITICAL ATTITUDES UPON CONTACT WITH NEGROES

In the preceding chapter, we indicated that the people in the New York projects differ somewhat from their counterparts in Newark. Thus, Koaltown has a relatively large percentage of Jewish people, while Sacktown has a group of comparatively well-educated housewives; the people in both of these projects are more liberal politically than the people in either Frankville or Bakerville. One may legitimately ask whether or not these differences provide an explanation for the differences in interracial contacts so far found to characterize the two types of projects.

For illustrative purposes, let us consider the degree of neighborly relationships between Negro and whites in the respective projects. We may further subdivide the data of Table 3 (see Table 4) so that we compare only the Jewish people in the various projects, or only the Catholics, or the relatively well educated, or those more liberal, or just the conservatives — or the people who are similar in other ways in religion, education, or political beliefs.

As Table 4 shows, it seems to make little difference what type of

TABLE 4. PERCENTAGES OF HOUSEWIVES IN DIFFERENT CLASSIFICATIONS
(OF POLITICAL ATTITUDES, EDUCATION, RELIGION) WHO HAVE NO
NEIGHBORLY RELATIONS WITH NEGRO PEOPLE IN THE PROJECT

	Integrated Interracial Projects		Segregated Bi-Racial Projects	
	Koaltown	Sacktown	Bakerville	Frankville
Political Attitudes				
Liberal	60% (35) *	36% (31)	100% (18)	92% (26)
Middle of road	59 (32)	22 (23)	100 (37)	95 (36)
Conservative	61 (31)	26 (35)	97 (45)	100 (38)
Education				
Only public school	68 (47)	39 (26)	100 (50)	93 (42)
Some high school	50 (28)	30 (30)	100 (33)	100 (34)
Completed high school or had some college	53 (15)	16 (31)	100 (14)	93 (14)
Religion				
Protestant	25 (4)	31 (16)	100 (23)	100 (16)
Catholic	58 (19)	38 (39)	98 (66)	98 (40)
Jewish	67 (72)	13 (23)	100 (7)	95 (41)

* The figures in parentheses represent the number of cases on which the percentage
is computed. In some cases the numbers are so small as to make the percentages relatively meaningless; they are included for consistency of presentation, only. The reader
should interpret them accordingly.

person you are, or what kind of background you have, or what type
of attitudes you possess; if you live in a segregated bi-racial project,
almost inevitably you have no neighborly relationships with the Negro people in the project. For example if the "politically liberal"
whites in the two types of projects are compared, we find that almost
all of those in the segregated projects (100 percent of 18; 92 percent
of 26) lack neighborly relations with Negro tenants, while this is
true of a considerably smaller percentage (60 percent of 35; 36 percent of 31) of liberals in the integrated projects. On the other hand,
even if your predispositions as a result of education, religion, and political attitudes do not favor interracial contact, you are likely to
have more contacts if you live in an integrated project than if you
were favorably predisposed and were living in a segregated project.

An illustration of this may be had by comparing political conservatives in the integrated projects with political liberals in the segregated
projects. The expected finding in terms of other research is that less
prejudiced attitudes (and presumably therefore more frequent interracial contact) would occur more often among those politically more
liberal than among those politically more conservative. However,
when the "liberals" are drawn from the segregated projects and the
"conservatives" from the integrated projects, the expected finding is
reversed. Whereas almost all of the "liberals" in the segregated proj-

ects (100 percent of 18 and 92 percent of 26) are entirely devoid of neighborly relations with Negro tenants, this can be said of only a considerably smaller percentage of the "conservatives" in the integrated projects (61 percent of 31 and 26 percent of 35).

Space prevents us from presenting tables in which interracial contacts of housewives who are equated simultaneously with respect to education, religion, and political attitudes in the two types of projects are compared. A typical example of what we find when making such comparisons will suffice. If politically conservative Catholic housewives with an elementary school education only are contrasted for the two types of projects, we obtain the following results: *None* of the 28 such housewives in the two segregated projects engages in neighborly activities with Negro women; in the integrated projects, however, 9 out of the 14 housewives with such characteristics have neighborly relations with Negro women.

Thus, even when similar groupings of people in the two types of projects are compared, it is clear that *the occupancy pattern markedly influences interracial contact. Moreover, its effects are of such strength as to reverse relationships often encountered in research studies between prejudiced attitudes and such factors as education, religion, or political attitudes.* This is not to assert that these factors have no influence whatever upon interracial contacts in these projects. From Table 4 it appears likely that under the conditions which characterize the integrated projects education is positively related to neighborly contacts (the effects of religion and political attitudes are not unequivocal). The relationship, however, expresses itself only in the integrated projects; or, in other words, only when the opportunities for interracial contact are favorable.

As yet, we have not discussed the consistent differences so far revealed between the two integrated projects, Sacktown and Koaltown. There is relatively less interracial contact between the housewives in Koaltown. Both the analysis of the data and our experiences in interviewing suggest an explanation. A large number of the Jewish housewives in Koaltown have had little schooling in the United States; they speak mostly Yiddish. The difference in language between them and the Negro tenants acts as a barrier to intimate communication and contact. Thirty-three out of the thirty-eight Jewish women in Koaltown who have not attended high school in this country have no neighborly relations with Negro women; in contrast, half of the more than 34 women who have gone to high school in this country do have such social relations. The Jewish people in Sacktown are, in contrast, rather young and well educated; they have no language barrier to overcome if they feel inclined to make conversation with their Negro neighbors while using the project laundry rooms or sitting together on the project benches.

In addition to the population dissimilarities, another factor probably influencing the differences obtained between Sacktown and Koaltown in interracial contact is their discrepancy in Negro-white ratios. The reader may recall that in Sacktown there are 70 Negro families to every 30 white families, while in Koaltown only 40 out of 100 families are Negro. Thus, more of the neighbors of the white women in Sacktown than in Koaltown are Negro. It is not unreasonable to assume that the greater number of opportunities in Sacktown for neighborly relationships with Negro families will result in more neighborly contacts. The reasoning here is similar to that which led us to expect differences in interracial contact between the integrated and the segregated projects. The lack of differences between Koaltown and Sacktown in the housewives' reports of the "likelihood of getting to know" Negro people in the project, however, is explainable by assuming that in both projects there are a sufficient number of Negro families to make it practically impossible to avoid having at least a superficial acquaintance with one or more Negro tenants.

CONTACTS BETWEEN NEGRO AND WHITE CHILDREN IN THE TWO TYPES OF PROJECTS

Twenty-four children in Sacktown and 24 children in Bakerville were interviewed; all were between the ages of 11 and 14. Half in each project were white, half Negro; half were girls, half boys.[11] We shall report here in summary form about shared spontaneous activities (initiated by the children themselves rather than by the school or the housing authority) with members of the other race and about visiting in the homes of members of the other race.

Shared Spontaneous Activities. Twenty of the 24 children interviewed in Sacktown share spontaneous activities, such as baseball, fishing, movies, and games, with members of the other race. These 20 are equally divided as to sex and race. In Bakerville, only 2 Negro children (a boy and a girl) assert they engage in such activities with white children, and in both cases the white children are outside the project. Neither of these Negro children engages in these activities

[11] The study of the children was conducted by Dorothy Barrett and Esther Rankin of the New York School of Social Work under the supervision of the Research Center for Human Relations. We shall present only a summary of their major findings. Their full study is on file at the library of the New York School of Social Work.

with white children in the project. While these differences are striking on the face of it, they appear even more significant when one takes into consideration the fact that all of the Negro and white children in Bakerville attend unsegregated schools and that some of the children from the different sections of the project go to the same school. As a result of their contacts in school all of the children have at least speaking acquaintances with members of the other race. Yet despite this, when they come home to the project, they share no activities. As one boy put it, "We play together at school and then return to our own side of the housing project and never see each other here."

Observation on four sunny days in each of the two projects corroborates the interview results. On all these days, Negro and white children in Sacktown were seen playing together freely and walking to and from the project arm-in-arm. During the four days spent in Bakerville, only one Negro child was seen playing on the side where white people lived and only one white child was seen playing on the side where the Negro people lived. These children turned out to be visitors from outside the housing project.

Home Visiting. In unsegregated Sacktown all but 2 of the 24 children interviewed visit in the homes of both their Negro and white friends in the project. Bakerville provides a sharp contrast: *none* of the 24 children interviewed visits in the homes of members of the other race in the project. One child, however, visits in the homes of Negro friends *outside* the project. He explained this by saying, "Nobody visits in the houses on the other side of the project."

In summary there seems little doubt that the interviews with children corroborate those with the housewives, and that taken together the two sets of interviews demonstrate clearly the marked effects of the occupancy pattern upon interracial contacts. We may be quite confident that *the likelihood of getting to know people of the other race and of having intimate contact with them is considerably greater in the integrated interracial than in the segregated bi-racial project.* The integrated project is, thus, considerably more successful in stimulating unprejudiced behavior toward Negroes among the white people in the project. Many more white people in the integrated than in the segregated projects violate, in actual behavior, the social prejudices and social customs which have the consequence of preventing intimate, equal-status contacts between Negroes and whites. In effect, living in the integrated projects produces a *behavioral* change with respect to race relations for many of the white people. This is a fact of considerable moral and social significance, for it is the *actions* of men rather than their thoughts that have direct social effects. Yet, since feelings and beliefs serve to predispose one to action, particularly in situations where there are no social pressures or other restraining influences, they are also of much importance. In a subsequent chapter we shall show to what extent the behavioral change is accompanied by a parallel *attitudinal* change.

CHAPTER VI

Social Norms Created by the
Occupancy Pattern

MAN is preeminently a *group* animal. From the moment of birth, he becomes a member simultaneously of many overlapping groups, such as the immediate family, the ethnic group, the neighborhood, the state. By adulthood, in a complex civilization such as ours, an individual has been a member of literally countless groups — teams, gangs, clubs, friendships, parties, classes — some of which are short-lived, some relatively enduring.[1]

Without cooperation on the part of its members, a group is not likely to obtain its objectives. In some social groups cooperation is maintained by expelling dissident group members; in others, by the threats of supernatural beings; in still others, by physical violence. In a complex society such as ours both formal and informal sanctions are employed — the police, the courts, the church, public scandal, gossip, etc. All function in one way or another to prevent the disruption of and to stimulate orderly cooperation among the members of a social group. However, the reliance on external sanctions as a guide to what the group considers to be socially desirable behavior is rarely efficient. Too much group energy must be spent in administering the group sanctions. Consider only how many policemen would be necessary to stop crime, if sole trust were placed in the external punishments of the courts or of public censure.

[1] By "group" we simply mean any two or more people who perceive themselves to be interdependent with respect to the achievement of their individual goals (cooperatively interdependent). Mutual friends, in terms of this definition, are "groups" if only in the sense that they perceive themselves to be interdependent with respect to their goals of friendship. The relationship of being neighbors is likely to lead to the perception of cooperative interdependence, if only in the limited sense of the implicit realization that "unless we all cooperate so that there will be peace and quiet, nobody will be free from trouble."

Assurance of cooperation comes primarily from the internalization of social norms or group standards. A "group standard" may be defined as the uniform set of values which group members are led to adopt as a consequence of their efforts to attain successfully the goals in relation to which they are mutually interdependent.[2] These values represent a group consensus (not necessarily "democratically" or formally arrived at) which helps to provide an orientation by which group members may coordinate their "activities" so as collectively to reach their goals. As G. H. Mead has pointed out in some detail,[3] cooperative coordination requires an anticipation of the reaction of others. With enduring coordination, Mead has indicated, these anticipated reactions of others tend to be internalized and generalized, the group standards operating (for most informal groups) through an internal, "generalized other." Thus, a measure of the nature of a group's standards is very frequently obtainable through the reactions anticipated to a given behavior by a member from other members.

A housing project may be seen as composed of many informal groups organized around various types of goals. These groups are intricately connected through the overlapping memberships of individuals within each group. Within this complex network it is likely that group standards or social norms will develop relevant to issues which are collectively important to the interconnected groups. In a society where prejudice is commonplace, interracial association will be such an issue. In Chapter III we have suggested that the social norms in the integrated projects will be more favorable to friendly interracial relations than will the corresponding social norms in the segregated projects. We hypothesized that this difference would follow as a consequence of the public sanction for friendly interracial relations implicit in the integrated occupancy pattern. In contrast, the social norm for race relations implicit in the segregated bi-racial project is that of avoidance of intimate social relations upon an equal-status basis. An additional factor which would work in the same direction is the comparatively greater number of cooperative relationships between Negroes and whites in the integrated projects arising out of the more frequent neighborly contacts between members of the two races.

From our interviews with housewives we got two types of data which permit us to make inferences about the nature of the social norms operating in the two types of projects: (1) the values of the

[2] For a more detailed discussion of group standards see L. Festinger, S. Schacter, and K. Back, *Social Pressures in Informal Groups* (Harper, 1950).

[3] See his *Mind, Self, and Society* (Univ. of Chicago, 1934).

housewives with respect to race relations and (2) the reactions the housewives anticipate from others if they are friendly with the Negro people in the project.

The values of the housewife with respect to association with Negroes. In the interviews with the white housewives we asked two questions to elicit value statements about intimate associations with the Negro people in the project. The questions were: "Are there any reasons why you think it might be better for you *not* to have much to do with the colored families in the project?" and "Are there any reasons why you think it might be better for you to *have* friends among the colored families in the project?"

A considerably higher percentage of the white women in Bakerville and Frankville (55 percent and 36 percent respectively) give "reasons" why it might be better *not* to have much to do with the colored families in the project than do the women in the integrated projects. The figures for Koaltown and Sacktown are 20 percent and 12 percent. Making the assumption, which evidence to be reported later supports, that the norms in the broader communities are much the same for all four projects, it seems likely that the obtained differences reflect real differences between the norms within the two types of projects. Considerably more people in the segregated projects (49 as contrasted with 11 in the integrated projects) develop or retain an ideology that "It's best for colored and white not to mix" or "We should stay on our side and they should stay on their side" or "It's best not to have anything to do with them." In addition there is more frequent spontaneous mention of social pressure not to mix from other whites in the segregated projects. Thus, one woman said, "They'd think you're crazy if you had a colored woman visit you in your home. They'd stare at you and there'd be a lot of talk." Another said, "I used to be good friends with a colored woman who worked with me at Westinghouse before I moved here. She lives in the other side of the project but I never have her over to my apartment — it just isn't done. Occasionally I go over and visit her." No instances of social pressures not to mix with Negro people were mentioned in the integrated projects.

In Sacktown 73 percent and in Koaltown 53 percent of the women indicate reasons for having friends among the Negro families in the project; in sharp contrast, only 19 percent of the women in Bakerville and 25 percent of them in Frankville believe it is desirable to be friendly with the Negro people. The majority of the reasons given in both types of projects are ideological in nature; they assert values of friendliness and neighborliness, values which they see as applying to the Negro people in the project. Thus, an elderly woman in Koaltown said, "Why not? I believe in being friendly with everybody. To me it makes no difference if they're white or black. Why shouldn't you be friendly with people?" Another woman in Sacktown responded to our question thus: "You should be neighborly with the people next door. If you get into trouble, they'll help you out and if they need something you should help them out."

Fifteen percent of the women in Sacktown and 10 percent in Koaltown, in comparison with 4 percent of the women in each of the two segregated projects, indicate social pressure to be friendly from the Negro people in the project. A young mother in Sacktown said, "They resent you if you're not friendly. You're liable to find yourself in plenty of trouble around here if you try to be snooty." Thus, the housewife in the integrated project is more likely to be exposed to direct social pressure to be friendly, while, on the other hand, the housewife in the segregated project is exposed to pressure not to be friendly.

In summary, the responses in the two types of projects are rather different to our questions asking for reasons for being friendly or not being friendly with the Negro people in the project. The majority of the housewives in the integrated projects think it is better to be friendly; this feeling reflects, for most of the housewives sharing it, values of neighborliness and nondiscrimination. These values, we have hypothesized, reflect the influence of the standards for behavior with respect to Negro neighbors which are implicit in the official policy of nonsegregation and in the ancient imperative to "love thy neighbor as thyself." In contrast, the policy of segregation appears to reinforce existing values favoring separation of the two races. Clearly then, we find the occupancy pattern associated with the ideology of the housewife with respect to race relations in the project; apparently it helps to determine the likelihood of her evaluating the idea of friendly relations with the Negro people in the project positively or negatively.

Anticipated reactions from others. Of all the informal sanctions which are employed to make member behavior conform to the social norms of the group, gossip and public notoriety are perhaps the most important. To avoid group hostility and to avoid being the objects of malicious gossip, people learn to anticipate how others will react if they behave in certain ways. These anticipations serve to guide the individual so that he conforms with the norms of the group.

Evidence previously presented indicated the differential social pressures directly felt by the housewives in the two types of projects with respect to being friendly with Negroes. The expected reactions of

others also act indirectly as a social pressure. We asked the housewife to indicate the reactions she anticipated from her husband, from
her friends in the project, and from the management staff if she were
friendly with Negro families. Table 5 presents the results in summary
form.

TABLE 5. PERCENTAGES OF HOUSEWIVES ANTICIPATING VARIOUS REACTIONS FROM
HUSBANDS, FRIENDS IN THE PROJECT, AND THE MANAGEMENT STAFF
IF FRIENDLY WITH COLORED FAMILIES

	Integrated Interracial Projects		Segregated Bi-Racial Projects	
	Koaltown	Sacktown	Bakerville	Frankville
From Husbands	(89) *	(75)	(88)	(81)
Favorable	52%	67%	24%	19%
Mixed or neutral	24	12	27	26
Unfavorable	24	21	41	49
Don't know	0	0	8	6
From Friends in Project ..	(91)	(73)	(88)	(82)
Favorable	39	55	3	5
Mixed or neutral	27	23	22	21
Unfavorable	24	14	65	47
Don't know	10	8	10	27
From Management Staff ..	(102)	(86)	(96)	(97)
Favorable	53	46	29	33
Mixed or neutral	5	12	13	6
Unfavorable	2	1	8	1
Don't know	40	41	50	60

* The figures in parentheses indicate the number of cases on which the percentage
figures in each section of the table are computed.

It is strikingly clear that the housewives in the integrated projects
anticipate more favorable reactions in all three categories than do the
housewives in the segregated projects. They expect favorable reactions, on the average, while the respondent in the segregated projects
typically expects disapproval from her husband and friends in the
project. In both types of projects, the management staff is seen as
being more approving than disapproving. However, in the segregated
projects the housewives report more often the feeling that they don't
know about the management's point of view. Most of the people anticipating favorable reactions from management in the segregated
projects indicate as their reason that the staff is interracial. If this
were not the case, it is probable that the contrasts between the two
types of projects with respect to the perception of management's attitude would be even greater than they are now. Having an interracial staff, one can assume, tends to counter the effects on the ten-

ants' perception of management which the occupancy pattern might be expected to create.

The reactions anticipated by the Negro housewives in the two types of project in general, though paralleling the differences found for the white housewives, are not so different from each other as are those of the white housewives in the two types of projects. The Negro housewives in all the projects anticipate relatively more favorable than unfavorable reactions to interracial association from their husbands, friends within the project, and management staff. However, the number anticipating favorable responses is consistently greater in the integrated projects. Further, more of the Negro housewives in the integrated projects expect the white people to favor friendly interracial relations than to oppose them; the opposite result is found in the segregated projects. These findings are as one would expect. The social norm for Negroes with respect to racial relations is generally to favor friendly interracial association; they want to break down rather than maintain segregation. However, in the segregated projects, partly as a defense against the insult of segregation, counter sentiments develop to a certain extent: "If they don't want to be friendly, we don't want to be friendly either." Similar results, to be reported in Chapter XI, are found with respect to attitudes toward interracial housing.

The values induced in children with respect to interracial association. Perhaps the most impressive evidence as to the effects of the occupancy pattern in creating guides for behavior comes from the interviews with the children in Sacktown and Bakerville. It is appropriate to recall that the children in Bakerville go to unsegregated elementary schools where Negro and white children mix freely. As a consequence of meeting in the school, they all have at least speaking acquaintances with members of the other race. Many of them play games together in school and belong to the same clubs. Yet in no single instance, among the children we interviewed in Bakerville, do they engage in any such activities with children of the other race living in the project.

The children implicitly understand that different standards regarding interracial association exist in the school and in the housing project. When their own sensitivities to these differences in social norms fail, their mothers obviously know how to impose restrictive behavior. It is interesting to note that in the few cases where children from Bakerville have social contacts with members of the other race after school hours, the children with whom they have contact do not live in the project. Social relations with members of the other race who live outside the project are apparently not so severe a threat to the social norms of the project as social relations across racial lines within the project community itself.

Some examples will illustrate the effects of social norms on children in Bakerville:

One twelve-year-old girl stated that she had made friends with a Negro girl at camp and she thought the girl was very nice. Both girls lived in the project but they never saw each other.

A Negro girl who feels that she is good friends with a number of white children states that she plays with them at school and goes to the movies with them, but "in the project, I have nothing to do with them."

A Negro boy complained: "We play together at school and then return to our own side of the housing project and never see each other here."

All of the 24 children interviewed in Bakerville state that the Negro and white adults in the housing project do not mix. A typical remark reflecting the ideology of separation was made by a white boy: "They have their own side to live on. We don't go to the other side and when they come over here there is trouble." From the interviews with the children, it is apparent that the parents play a role in reinforcing this ideology. Thus one boy said: "My mother doesn't like Negroes and won't let me go around with them. She punishes me if I play with them." A white girl said her mother did not want her to visit Negroes, but she did not know the reason.

In contrast, all but two of the children interviewed in Sacktown say the Negro and white adults get along well together. Typically, when asked to express their parents' attitudes, they reply, "They see no differences between Negroes and whites."

Thus, the interviews with both children and housewives provide essentially the same results. Differences in the occupancy pattern are found to accompany differences in expectations as to how one should behave to achieve social approval; these expectations tend to become rationalized and internalized in the form of values concerning race relations. As the evidence of the preceding chapter has indicated, these values and expectations serve as a guide to behavior and influence interracial relations within the project to a considerable degree. *The guide for behavior to the person living in an integrated project is that of friendly interracial association; the standard implicit in the segregated pattern is that of avoidance, with the connotation that interracial association brings trouble or that it is socially degrading.*

CHAPTER VII

Social Norms and Social Relations within the Project

SOCIAL NORMS WITHIN THE PROJECT

THE poet John Donne has stated that "No man is an Illand, intire of it selfe." So, too, no project exists in complete isolation. It exists in a community and the attitudes in the community toward interracial relations have effects on the people in the project. This is why several questions in the interview were aimed at the reactions of relatives and friends outside the projects to friendly contacts by the white house-wives with Negro people.

From Table 6 it is clear that in all of the projects considerably more housewives anticipated that their friends in the broader community would disapprove, rather than approve, of their being friendly with the Negro tenants. However, in both Koaltown and Sacktown, a somewhat higher percentage reported having friends who would approve. While we have no systematic evidence on the point, one possible explanation of this finding might be that the housewives in these projects more frequently reject and are rejected by former friends who disapprove of their association with Negroes. Thus, one Sacktown housewife said, "I have lost a lot of my old friends who wouldn't want to visit me because I am neighborly with some of the Negro people here. But I've also made a lot of new ones." Another woman exclaimed, "They wouldn't be my friends for long if I knew they were prejudiced."

However, one cannot select one's relatives. All of the housewives in the four projects who mentioned relatives in answer to the question, "Are there any people or groups like relatives and friends who care one way or the other about whether you're friendly with colored families?" said their relatives would disapprove.

71

TABLE 6. PERCENTAGES OF HOUSEWIVES ANTICIPATING VARIOUS REACTIONS FROM
FRIENDS OUTSIDE THE PROJECT IF FRIENDLY WITH COLORED FAMILIES

Anticipated Reaction	Integrated Interracial Projects		Segregated Bi-Racial Projects	
	Koaltown (98)	Sacktown (80)	Bakerville (88)	Frankville (91)
Favorable	9%	25%	0%	3%
Mixed or neutral	26	28	25	23
Unfavorable	54	38	56	55
Don't know	11	9	19	19

A comparison of the anticipated reactions of people within the project with those of people outside the project (compare Table 6 with Table 5 in the preceding chapter) provides clear indication that the social norms in the integrated projects will be more favorable to friendly interracial relations than will the pressures to which the white tenants are exposed from outside the project. While the parallel comparison for the segregated projects is not entirely clear, there appears to be relatively little difference between reactions anticipated from friends inside and those from outside the project community.

For the housewife in the segregated project, the reaction of the broader community presents no problem since she has little contact with the Negro people and the standard for behavior implicit in the policy of separating Negro and white families does not suggest such contact. In contrast, the housewife in an integrated project experiences a dilemma in this respect. As one of them said: "I'm very friendly with the (Negro) lady next door; we're in and out of each other's place all the time. That's it. A problem comes up when my relatives, especially my mother-in-law, visit. They don't like the idea of me living next door to Negroes. You know my friend sometimes just pops in. Well, I don't want to hurt my friend — I got to get along with my mother-in-law — it's a problem all right."

Several consequences appear to result directly from the cross pressures which face the housewife in the integrated project. First of all, she is more aware of the interracial aspects of the project than her counterpart in the segregated project. Whether her attitude toward it is positive or negative, the interracial composition of the project is more prominent in her thinking. During the course of the interview (before the interviewer asked any questions specifically related to the Negro people) the housewives in the integrated projects spontaneously mentioned the Negro group or the interracial aspects of the project both earlier and more frequently than did the women in the segre-

gated projects. One woman in Sacktown who was particularly enthusiastic about the interracial aspects of the project provides an
apt illustration. In response to an initial general inquiry concerning
her reactions to the project, she stated, "It's wonderful. I never
thought I would like living so close to Negroes but it's been a wonderful experience for me and my children." Twenty-one percent of
the women in Koaltown and 35 percent in Sacktown spoke about
the interracial aspects of the project at the first opportunity; for
Bakerville and Frankville, the corresponding figures are 6 percent
and 8 percent. Only 10 percent in Bakerville and 22 percent in Frankville spontaneously talked about the interracial aspects of the project
at least twice before questions were asked about the Negro people; in
sharp contrast are the figures in the integrated projects — Koaltown
41 percent and Sacktown 45 percent.

In interpreting this spontaneous mention of Negro tenants, we must
keep in mind the interviewing context. The interviewer, a stranger
from outside the project, in a sense symbolizes the external community and thus is likely to evoke responses about matters which are
of greatest concern to the housewife in her relationship to this outside community. If this is true, it follows from our findings that, in
their relation to the broader community, interracial association is a
matter of concern to more white housewives in integrated than in
segregated projects.

SOCIAL RELATIONS WITHIN THE PROJECT

In Chapter III we have suggested that an issue which is of concern to a number of people in common frequently draws these people
closer together. Their mutual concern provides a common bond of
experience, a basis of intimate conversation. It results in increased
socialization in the course of working out solutions to the problems
which the issue represents, and gives those concerned an opportunity
to find support for their opinions. Thus, the housewife in Sacktown
who faces the dilemma of a prejudiced mother-in-law and a friendly
Negro neighbor who pops in and out is not alone in her conflict;
many of her white neighbors face similar problems. It is only natural,
since no conventional, well-established customs exist for the handling
of these problematic social situations (certainly none of the standard
books of social etiquette provide ready answers) that these women
share their experiences in searching for a satisfactory solution.

There are, potentially, many collective issues about which residents
in a housing project may be drawn together. Interracial association

constitutes only one of many. This, of course, makes it difficult to determine whether our results on the social cohesiveness of the various project communities are a function solely of the differences between the social norms within and those without the project.

The second section of Table 3, presented in Chapter V, indicated that there are considerably more neighborly activities (visiting with one another, helping one another, going out together, and informal or club activities) among the women in the integrated than in the segregated projects. These activities involve fairly close and intimate relationships and may be taken as a crude measure of the social cohesiveness of the project. In Table 7 the results of another measure reflective of cohesiveness are presented, namely, the number of close friends the housewife has within the project. It is clear from this that the women in Koaltown and Sacktown, by and large, have more close friends in their projects than do the housewives in Bakerville and Frankville.

TABLE 7. PERCENTAGES OF HOUSEWIVES INDICATING A SPECIFIC NUMBER OF CLOSE FRIENDS WITHIN THE PROJECT*

Number of Close Friends	Integrated Interracial Projects		Segregated Bi-Racial Projects	
	Koaltown (86)	Sacktown (85)	Bakerville (94)	Frankville (94)
None	26%	18%	34%	32%
1–4	39	37	44	42
5 or more	35	45	22	26

* Some housewives did not indicate a specific number of close friends; these responses are not included.

When asked to describe what the people in their project are like, the housewives in the integrated projects draw much more favorable pictures of their co-tenants, white as well as Negro, than do their counterparts in the segregated projects. In Koaltown 60 percent and in Sacktown 70 percent use such phrases as: "They're very nice," "Everyone has a friendly 'hello'," "People are very neighborly here." In contrast only about a third of the women in the segregated projects have positive remarks to make about each other. The latter are almost as apt to make a hostile as a friendly remark; for every one woman in the integrated projects who judges her neighbors unfavorably there are 5 to 7 women who evaluate them positively.

It seems likely that the greater friendliness which characterizes the relationships of housewives in the integrated projects results, in some measure, from the cross pressures to which they are exposed. Partly as a defense and partly as a means of solidifying themselves in the face of outside disapproval, the housewives have been drawn closer together with the resulting social gain of increased project cohesiveness. A complimentary loss of some friends outside the project might be expected, but actually this does not occur. It is true that housewives in the integrated projects report losing some former friends who are prejudiced but they also report gaining new friends. The results indicate no difference between the housewives in the two types of projects in number of close friends outside the projects. These results in conjunction with the results of Table 7 indicate that altogether, inside and outside the project, the average white housewife in the integrated project is likely to have more white, as well as Negro, friends than the average white housewife in the segregated biracial project.

However, there are relatively fewer women in the integrated projects who have more friends outside the project than within the project. In Bakerville 67 percent and in Frankville 73 percent of the women have fewer friends inside than outside their project; the corresponding figures for Sacktown and Koaltown are 57 percent and 49 percent, respectively. These data may be taken as further evidence of the greater social cohesiveness of the integrated when compared with the segregated project.

A final measure which may be taken as indicative of project cohesiveness is given by the percentage of housewives in the various projects who report belonging to an organization inside the project (Table 8). More housewives in Sacktown and Koaltown, in comparison with those in the segregated projects, belong to such organizations. However, more of them belong to outside organizations also. Our interviews unfortunately do not provide us with an explanation of this latter result. However, it is evident that the finding that more housewives in the integrated projects belong to outside organizations does not provide an adequate explanation of the finding that more also belong to project organizations. Even when one considers people who are members of a project organization only, the difference between the integrated and segregated projects is significant.

In Koaltown there is a particularly active tenants' organization, a fact that in part reflects the manager's ability to arouse tenant enthusiasm. This may account for some of the difference shown in Table 8 between the two New York projects, but it does not seem adequate

to explain the differences between the integrated and segregated projects. The relative lack of tenant activities in Newark probably reflects, in part, the social effects of the segregated occupancy pattern.
In the segregated projects there are central social facilities open to
both Negroes and whites. Many white tenants, in the atmosphere of
segregation, shun these facilities and thus generally limit the possibilities of making friends within the project, even with members of
their own race.

TABLE 8. PERCENTAGES OF HOUSEWIVES WHO REPORTED BEING A MEMBER OF AN
ORGANIZATION INSIDE OR OUTSIDE THE PROJECT

	Integrated Interracial Projects		Segregated Bi-Racial Projects	
	Koaltown (102)	Sacktown (90)	Bakerville (100)	Frankville (100)
Not a member of either	44%	69%	92%	74%
Member of an outside organization only	15	8	4	15
Member of an inside organization only	25	14	4	9
Member of both	16	9	0	2

To sum up, we have shown that the social norms of the integrated
projects with respect to racial relations are more divergent from the
norms of the broader community than are the corresponding norms
in the segregated bi-racial projects. As a consequence of this diver-
gency, the housewife finds herself exposed to various cross pressures.
These cross pressures make the issue of interracial relations an area
of fairly prominent interest and concern. We have hypothesized that
an issue of common concern to a number of interacting people is likely
to draw these people more closely together — in the case of integrated
housing, partly as a defense against social disapproval by the broader
community of close interracial contact within the project, and partly
as a means of working out solutions to difficult social problems. The
results bear out this hypothesis: *the integrated projects are characterized by a friendlier, more cohesive social atmosphere.* The white
housewives in the integrated projects know each other better, like
each other better, and do more things together; in other words, not
only do they have closer relationships with the Negro people but they
also have closer relationships with the other white people in their
project than do their counterparts in the segregated bi-racial projects. There was no evidence to indicate that this gain in social co-

hesiveness of the integrated project results in or from an over-all loss of friendships with people outside the project. On the other hand, there is some evidence to indicate that the housewife in the segregated project by shunning activities in which Negro tenants may partici- pate incurs a loss in opportunities for friendly social relationships with members of her own race as well.

CHAPTER VIII

Attitudes toward Negro People
in the Project

So FAR, our results have clearly indicated that the integrated in contrast with the segregated bi-racial project creates more opportunities for close contact between races, a social atmosphere more conducive to friendly interracial relations, and a more closely knit project community. It is not unnatural to expect that these differences between the two types of projects will be the source of differences in attitudes. Many of the white tenants in the integrated projects have had the kinds of experiences with Negro neighbors which could result in more favorable attitudes; few of the tenants in the segregated projects have had such experiences.

Such change as occurs may be limited to the individual's attitudes toward the Negro people in the project or it may be generalized, affecting his attitudes toward Negro people in general. It may even change his attitudes toward other racial or religious groups which are objects of prejudice. In this chapter, we shall examine the effects upon attitudes toward the Negro people in the project; in two subsequent chapters, we shall see what generalized changes result.[1]

Implicit in our expectation of a change in attitudes toward Negroes is the assumption that the more favorable social norms and the greater frequency of contact will be accompanied in the integrated project by more friendly relationships between Negro and white tenants. As we have indicated in Chapter III, this assumption runs

[1] It is particularly relevant, at this point, to recall a basic assumption which underlies the interpretation of differences between the two types of projects, namely, the differences in attitudes between the people in the two types of projects reflect differences in their experiences while living in their respective projects. In other words, the differences are due to the occupancy pattern rather than to differences in religion, political attitudes, education, etc.

78

counter to that of the proponents of "White Supremacy," who expect that if Negroes and whites are "forced" into intimate, equal-status contacts racial strife will ensue. Table 9 summarizes data which bear directly upon the assumption of an inevitable basic antagonism between members of the two races.[2]

TABLE 9. PERCENTAGES OF HOUSEWIVES REPORTING VARIOUS
RELATIONS WITH NEGRO PEOPLE IN THE PROJECT

Type of Relations	Integrated Interracial Projects		Segregated Bi-Racial Projects	
	Koaltown (102)	Sacktown (90)	Bakerville (100)	Frankville (101)
Friendly	60%	69%	6%	4%
Accommodative	24	14	5	1
Mixed	7	11	2	3
None	5	0	87	88
Bad	4	6	0	4

The results demonstrate that the relationships between Negro people and the white housewives in the integrated projects are preponderantly friendly, while in the segregated projects most housewives do not have any relationships with the Negro people in the project. Many women in the integrated projects made statements of this nature (*friendly relations*): "We get along beautifully. They're really wonderful. When I was sick, Mrs. Jones across the hall noticed it and she came in and helped. She used to bring food in and go shopping for me. A lot of white people wouldn't do that for you." Or: "They're nice to get along with. They treat me fine. They're the same as everybody else." The *accommodative relationship* is characterized by such remarks as: "I've had no trouble. They mind their own business, or they smile and say 'good morning.' But with me it's 'hello and goodbye.' I don't bother much with people here." The *mixed reaction* is evidenced by phrases like "Some are nice, but some are nasty." None

[2] There is, of course, a close relationship between the results summarized in Table 9 and those summarized in Table 3 (Chapter V). However, the data presented in the two tables have been derived independently of each other. Table 3 summarizes the related responses to question 26 (see Appendix F) which asks specifically about various types of neighborly contacts, while Table 9 summarizes the ratings of coders of the housewives' relationship with Negro neighbors. The ratings of the coders are based upon the housewives' responses to question 9, which asks general questions about the Negro people in the project. Table 9, in effect, gives a measure of the amicability of the housewife's relationship with Negroes, as viewed by the housewife, independently of its extent. One would expect a correlation between extent and amicability but it is not inevitable that a housewife who engages in a neighborly relationship has a friendly view of this relationship.

of the instances of *bad relations* were characterized by physical violence; they took the form of an intense discomfort or dislike. Thus, one housewife in an integrated project, who was rated as having bad relations with the Negro tenants, said, "I've never liked them. I guess they know it and have told their kids. They call me 'white trash' whenever they see me. I have to keep careful watch on my kids or else the colored kids will gang up on them."

The interviews with the Negro housewives give much the same results as presented in Table 9. More than half of the Negro housewives in each of the integrated projects report friendly relations with the white women in the project; on the other hand, somewhat over 80 percent in each of the segregated projects report no social relations with white women. Though there are instances of dislike and discomfort in both types of projects, the "trouble" which opponents of interracial housing expect to arise does not occur in well-managed projects. *Neither the segregated nor the integrated interracial projects that we have studied are characterized by any interracial strife.*

We may make several inferences from the preponderance of positive relationships observed in the integrated projects. There seems to be no doubt, for one thing, that the Negro tenants fail to conform to the stereotypes or rationales for prejudiced feelings frequently held by whites. If they did conform, it is doubtful that the housewives interviewed in the integrated projects could have reported such satisfactory interracial experiences. Moreover, it is clear not only that the behavior of the Negro tenants fails to conform to stereotype, but also that this nonconformity will become more apparent to white tenants in integrated than in segregated projects. We might expect, further, that the greater degree of contact with "nonconforming" Negroes in the integrated projects will result in an increased perception of their positive attributes and a diminution in the frequency of negative stereotypes. Conversely, the lack of relationships in the segregated projects might be expected to perpetuate existing stereotypes and not provide the experience for the perception of positive attributes.

A check on this point is provided by the data presented in Table 10, which summarizes positive and negative attributes respectively ascribed to the Negro people in the project. It is apparent that more housewives in the integrated projects than in the segregated projects ascribe positive attributes to the Negro people, while the reverse is true for negative attributes.

It is interesting to note that, of the people mentioning positive attributes, relatively more in the integrated projects mention attributes such as helpfulness that are related to neighborliness. Other attributes

mentioned frequently are politeness, respectability, sociability, friendliness, and cheerfulness. The negative attributes mentioned by housewives in the segregated projects are, for the most part, the usual
stereotypes; for example, they say Negroes are "impulsive," "primi-
tive," "troublemakers," "dangerous," etc. In the integrated projects,
one of the most frequently mentioned negative attributes is quite
uncommon, that is, the one labeled "inferiority complex" about prejudice. One housewife in Sacktown expressed her feeling this way:

TABLE 10. PERCENTAGES OF HOUSEWIVES WHO ASCRIBE VARIOUS ATTRIBUTES TO
NEGRO PEOPLE IN THE PROJECT*

Attribute Most Frequently Mentioned	Integrated Interracial Projects		Segregated Bi-Racial Projects	
	Koaltown (102)	Sacktown (90)	Bakerville (100)	Frankville (101)
Positive Attributes				
Helpful, do you favors, good neighbors	18%	28%	1%	0%
Polite, respectable	20	14	11	7
Sociable, friendly, cheerful	15	33	6	11
Try to improve themselves	3	17	3	3
They're people, human beings	36	17	19	27
No positive attributes mentioned	27	17	54	52
Negative Attributes				
Low-class, noisy, rowdy, impulsive, primitive, drink a lot	14	9	33	25
Inadequate parental control; children are destructive	13	18	17	23
"Inferiority complex" about prejudice	12	19	1	2
Troublemakers, aggressive, dangerous	13	10	36	31
No negative attributes mentioned	61	68	46	53

* Percentages may add up to more than 100% because some housewives mentioned
more than one attribute.

"They're extremely sensitive. They'll jump down your throat if you
even look like you might be prejudiced." Another said, "They're
very suspicious of whites. They think we're trying to take over their
project." Someone else commented: "They have it in for whites.
They've been beaten down and hurt for so long that they're out for
their revenge." It would seem likely that this attribution of "sensitivity" or "inferiority complex" to Negroes, implies more of an ap-
preciation of the Negro as a person than is true of the more usual

negative attributes. It recognizes in him understandable psychological characteristics and a human motivation which, although having troublesome consequences, allow for the possibility of empathy.

Additional evidence that the behavior of the Negro people in the projects was "pretty much the same" as that of the white people in the projects was obtained from answers to the question: "Are they (the Negro people in the project) pretty much the same as the white people who live here or are they different?" In Sacktown, 84 percent say, "They're the same"; in Koaltown, 75 percent; in Bakerville, 63 percent; and in Frankville, 52 percent. Thus, although the figures are significantly higher for the integrated projects, the majority of the housewives in all the projects feel the Negro people are pretty much the same as the white people. It is apparent, however, that the housewives in the integrated projects have had more opportunity to perceive this essential similarity. In their reasons for saying that the Negroes were "pretty much the same," they offer somewhat more frequently such statements as: "Well, they just behave the same way the white people do. They're nice and friendly, just like anybody else."

Table 11 summarizes material in addition to that presented in Table 10 regarding the conceptions of Negroes held by the housewives. It indicates that the overwhelming majority of women in the integrated developments respect the Negro tenants; in contrast, there are in the segregated projects almost as many housewives who feel that the Negro people are inferior as there are who feel that they are equal to the white. Many more of the housewives in the integrated projects make statements such as these: "They're very nice; they have beautiful homes"; "A lot of them are nicer than the white peo-

TABLE 11. PERCENTAGES OF HOUSEWIVES WHO HOLD THE NEGRO PEOPLE IN THE PROJECT IN DIFFERENT DEGREES OF ESTEEM

Degree of Esteem	Integrated Interracial Projects		Segregated Bi-Racial Projects	
	Koaltown (102)	Sacktown (90)	Bakerville (100)	Frankville (101)
Respect Negroes living in the project; view them as equal to white people in the project	72%	79%	43%	39%
Feel Negroes are inferior; characterize them as low-class, childish, primitive, etc.	11	13	37	35
Neutral or ambivalent	17	8	20	26

TABLE 12. PERCENTAGES OF HOUSEWIVES WITH DIFFERENT FEELINGS TOWARD
NEGRO PEOPLE LIVING IN THE PROJECT

Feeling Expressed	Integrated Interracial Projects		Segregated Bi-Racial Projects	
	Koaltown (102)	Sacktown (90)	Bakerville (100)	Frankville (98)
Like Negroes in the project and desire to be friendly ..	42%	60%	9%	5%
Have mixed or reserved feelings, not friendly, not avoidant	30	12	12	27
Have avoidant feelings toward Negroes	28	28	79	68

ple; when I was sick the lady across the hall came in and cooked soup"; "They're just the same as the white people here; except for color, there's no difference." On the other hand, considerably more women in the segregated projects make statements which imply that Negroes are inferior. Thus, one woman in Bakerville said: "They can't help it, but they act like children . . . the way they like to show off and have a good time." Another said: "Well, they're different from white people. I don't know how to say it but you know what I mean. It's something in them that makes them wild and uncivilized."

In Table 12 some information about the feelings of the housewife toward the Negro people in the project are summarized.[3] In the integrated projects there are approximately two housewives who like and want to be friendly to Negro tenants to every one housewife who wishes to avoid contact with Negroes; in the segregated developments there is approximately only one who wishes to be friendly to every ten who wish to avoid relationships. These marked differences give evidence of a considerable reduction in prejudiced feelings toward Negro tenants among the housewives in the integrated projects.

Psychoanalysis has shown that man's beliefs frequently serve as defenses or justifications for his feelings. Under attack the beliefs may shift or change, but as long as the underlying feelings are not

[3] Comparable results are obtained from the interviews with the Negro housewives. Thirty-four of the 49 Negro housewives interviewed in the New York projects view the white people with respect; however, only 25 of them professed a desire for close, friendly relations with the white women in the project. In contrast only 8 of the 50 Negro women in the segregated projects expressed respect for the white people in the project; only 5 of the 50 indicated a desire for close, friendly relations. (Most are noncommittal rather than contemptuous or avoidant.)

altered new beliefs to justify the feelings will soon develop. So too, evidence is accumulating that in the development of prejudice feelings are often prior to beliefs. Thus, Blake and Dennis have concluded from their investigation of the development of stereotypes that "the young white child acquires first of all a generally unfavorable attitude toward the Negro, which makes him unwilling to attribute toward the Negro any 'good' traits. With increasing age and experience, the child gradually learns to apply the adult stereotype . . . ."[4] One would, thus, anticipate that the stereotypes or the conceptions the housewife has of the Negro are likely to change more readily than the feelings which underlie them.

A comparison of Tables 11 and 12 from this point of view is highly suggestive, though (in itself, without additional research) far from conclusive. As may be seen from the tables a higher proportion of the housewives in all four projects hold the Negro tenants in high esteem than desire to be friendly with them. The differences between the housewives in the two types of projects are somewhat greater with respect to "friendly feelings" (Table 12) than in regard to "esteem" (Table 11). A number of interpretations of this result are possible. One interpretation would support the notion that "feelings" are more basic than "beliefs," that beliefs are a more superficial layer of the personality than feelings. According to this interpretation a change in beliefs is a necessary but not always a sufficient condition for a change in feelings.

In other words, even the superficial contacts between Negroes and whites in the segregated projects might be enough to destroy the belief of many housewives that Negroes are basically inferior, whereas more intimate experiences would be necessary to produce friendly feelings. This interpretation would explain both why relatively more people in all four projects reject the notion of inferiority than desire friendly relations and also why the differences between the housewives in the integrated and segregated projects are greater for "feelings" than for "beliefs." An alternative explanation that feelings change more readily than beliefs would explain the latter but not the former.

The statements of some of the housewives in the integrated projects who felt that the Negroes in the project were equal to the whites but who nevertheless felt inclined to avoid them also provide insight into the question of the primacy of beliefs and feelings. Statements such as these were typical: "I don't know why I feel this way . . .

[4] R. Blake and W. Dennis, "The Development of Stereotypes Concerning the Negro," *Journal of Abnormal and Social Psychology*, 1943, 38:525-31.

but I just don't like my boys to be playing with so many colored children." "I know it's wrong but the thought of having colored women in for coffee the way some of the other women do . . . it just upsets me."

In Chapter V we noted that living in the integrated projects produces a behavioral change with respect to race relations for many of the white people, a change which is in the direction of more frequent interracial association. While the evidence is far from conclusive, there is a suggestion that behavior changes more readily than attitudes. In Chapter V we noted that 49 percent of the housewives in Koaltown and 77 percent in Sacktown indicate that they know at least one Negro in the project "pretty well." Table 12, which gives a measure of the housewife's desire for friendly, social relations with the Negro people in the project (Koaltown, 42 percent; Sacktown, 60 percent), when contrasted with the preceding figures suggests that some women are less prejudiced in behavior than in their feelings. This discrepancy in behavior and attitudes may reflect the effect of the social norms in the integrated projects as a guide and pressure to unprejudiced behavior.

THE EFFECTS OF THE OCCUPANCY PATTERN VERSUS THE EFFECTS OF RELIGION, EDUCATION, AND POLITICAL ATTITUDES UPON ATTITUDES TOWARD THE NEGRO PEOPLE IN THE PROJECT

In Chapter III we indicated the necessity of considering the possibility that differences between the people in the two types of projects with respect to religion, education, and/or political attitudes might adequately explain the contrasts in interracial contact and attitudes revealed by our data. Clearly, if these factors provide an adequate explanation of our results, little causal significance could be attributed to experiences associated with the occupancy pattern. In Chapter V our analysis demonstrated that the marked differences in the number of intimate, social contacts between Negroes and whites in the two types of projects could not be explained by dissimilarities in religion, education, or political attitudes; the most reasonable explanation was the difference in the occupancy pattern.[5] It is appropriate at this point to examine also our attitudinal data

[5] From other research one would, of course, expect these striking contrasts in interracial contacts due to the occupancy pattern to result in differences in attitudes. To a certain extent, after the demonstration of the contact dissimilarities in the two types of project, the burden of proof shifts. If no difference in attitudes were revealed, one could seriously raise the question: "How, in the light of the large differences in social experience with Negroes could one obtain results which did not indicate considerable dissimilarities in attitudes?"

to see whether or not the results reported earlier in this chapter are explainable by factors other than the occupancy pattern.

For illustrative purposes, let us consider some of the data presented in Table 12. (The results are very much the same no matter what attitudinal measure is analyzed.) We may subdivide the data of Table 12 (see Table 13) so that we compare only the liberals in the various projects, only the relatively well educated, the Catholics only, just those who have not gone to high school, or people who are similar in religion, education, and political beliefs.

TABLE 13. PERCENTAGES OF HOUSEWIVES IN DIFFERENT CLASSIFICATIONS (OF POLITICAL ATTITUDES, EDUCATION, RELIGION) WHO HAVE FRIENDLY FEELINGS TOWARD NEGRO PEOPLE IN THE PROJECT

	Integrated Interracial Projects		Segregated Bi-Racial Projects	
	Koaltown	Sacktown	Bakerville	Frankville
Political Attitudes				
Liberal	31% (35)*	72% (32)	0% (18)	17% (24)
Middle of road	53 (32)	65 (23)	19 (37)	3 (36)
Conservative	48 (31)	46 (35)	4 (45)	0 (38)
Education				
Only public school	32 (47)	50 (26)	8 (50)	5 (40)
Some high school	61 (28)	48 (31)	9 (33)	0 (35)
Completed high school or had some college .	53 (15)	84 (31)	7 (14)	14 (14)
Religion				
Protestant ...	50 (4)	75 (16)	0 (23)	0 (16)
Catholic	53 (19)	36 (39)	6 (66)	0 (40)
Jewish	36 (75)	78 (23)	43 (7)	10 (40)

* Figures in parentheses indicate the number of cases on which the percentage figures have been computed. In some cases, the numbers are so small as to make the percentages relatively meaningless.

From Table 13, it is clear that it is of little import whether the housewife is educated or not, is liberal or conservative, Catholic or Jewish; if she lives in a segregated bi-racial project she is unlikely to have warm positive feelings toward the Negro people in the project. On the other hand, even if her predispositions as a result of education, religion, and political attitudes are unfavorable, she is more likely to have friendly feelings toward the Negro people if she lives in an integrated project than if, though predisposed to friendly feelings, she were living in a segregated project. (The figure for the Jewish people in Bakerville runs counter to this statement. We have no ready explanation of this single exception. However, the number of cases on which it is based is quite small; as a consequence probably not much confidence should be placed in it.)

If we compare people in the two types of projects who are equated simultaneously with respect to education, religion, and political attitudes we obtain similar results. Thus, for example, if Catholic housewives who are politically conservative and who have had only an elementary school education are contrasted, we obtain the following results: *none* of the 28 such housewives in the segregated projects profess positive feelings toward the Negro people in the project; in the integrated projects, however, 7 out of the 14 housewives with such characteristics indicate these feelings. Or if we parallel Jewish housewives in the two types of projects who are politically "middle-of-the-road" and who have had some high school education, we get similar findings: only 1 out of 8 such housewives in the segregated, as compared with 6 out of 8 in the integrated, projects have friendly feelings toward the Negro tenants. While the numbers are small, the evidence is cumulative; it makes no difference which equated groups of people are chosen, the findings are similar.

Thus, even when similar groupings of people in the two types of project are compared, it is strikingly clear that, as was the case with interracial contact, attitudes toward the Negro people in the project are markedly influenced by the occupancy pattern; *the effects of experiences associated with the occupancy pattern are stronger than the effects of such factors as education, religion, or political attitudes.*

We have not in the preceding analysis discussed the differences in attitudes between Koaltown and Sacktown, though it is evident that some significant differences do exist between the two projects. The explanation of the differences is the same as that offered during the discussion of interracial contact in Chapter V. More of the Jewish people in Koaltown are relatively unassimilated; they speak mostly Yiddish and have not established intimate contact with the Negro people in the project. Only 5 of the 38 Jewish women in Koaltown who have not gone to high school in this country have positive feelings (the largest group of these people are reserved rather than avoidant). Of the other Jewish women in Koaltown more than half profess friendly feelings. The Jewish people in Sacktown, on the other hand, are rather well educated and have no language barrier or old-world habits to overcome in establishing contacts and friendly feelings. In addition, the greater frequency of intimate neighborly contacts in Sacktown, which in part seems to be due to its higher ratio of Negro families, could be expected to provide more of the experiences with Negroes which can be counted upon to produce favorable attitudinal changes.

ATTITUDES OF THE CHILDREN IN THE TWO TYPES OF PROJECTS

Although the data on the racial attitudes of the children are rather scanty, they indicate findings which correspond to those found with the adults.

In Sacktown, 18 of the 24 children interviewed, 8 boys and 10 girls, said there were no differences between Negro and white people. Ten of these were Negro children and 8 were white children. One white boy said, "They are just like us when you really know them." One said, "Some Negro people are better than some white people; it depends on the person." In Bakerville, 12 of the 24 children interviewed, 5 boys and 7 girls, said there were no differences between Negro and white people. Ten of these children were Negro children and only 2 were white children. None of them were white boys.

In summary, the interviews with the children and the housewives, white and Negro, have indicated that the attitudes of the residents in the integrated projects are considerably less prejudiced than those of the people in the segregated bi-racial projects. We have examined such factors as religion, education, and political attitudes to see whether, singly or in combination, they provide a satisfactory explanation of these attitudinal differences. Clearly they do not. It seems reasonable to assume therefore that these differences are causally related to the occupancy pattern as follows: The integrated project, by creating more opportunities for close, social contacts between Negroes and whites and by stimulating a social atmosphere more conducive to friendly racial relations, exposes its tenants to the kinds of experiences which are likely to change prejudicial attitudes. In contrast, the segregated project does little to stimulate the experiences necessary to the disruption of prejudices. Though we have not presented any direct measure of attitudinal change, the differences between attitudes in the two types of projects may be taken as a crude index of the change in attitudes among the housewives in the integrated projects. Despite the roughness of the indicator, it is evident that the change has been marked in many of the housewives studied.

CHAPTER IX

Attitudes toward Negro People in General

IT HAS been frequently observed that attitude changes of the type described in the previous chapter may have little generality. Thus, Marie Jahoda has written: "The organizer of an interracial camp who has watched members of different groups drawing closer and judging each other on an individual basis rather than in terms of group membership, sometimes is shocked to find that some of the participants return to their communities and continue a pattern of strictly segregated life. Trade union officials in Detroit who had consistently advocated and implemented a policy of nonsegregation and educated their membership to the acceptance of this principle were disturbed to learn that some of their staunchest union members had actively participated in the race riots in 1943. . . . Such apparent inconsistencies are all too familiar to the practitioner in the field of intergroup relations who has often been discouraged by the discovery that changes produced in one situation have little effect on behavior in another context." [1]

In this chapter, we are going to present data on attitudes toward the Negro people in general. These data will provide a partial answer to the question of the generality of attitude changes which result from experiences of living in different types of interracial housing projects. In some respects, the data may not be satisfactory for the purpose since they were all collected in one context — the interviewing situation. This may operate to enhance the apparent generality of attitude changes.

The interviewers, at the conclusion of each of their interviews, made judgments about the attitudes of the housewife they had just finished interviewing. They rated her respect and friendliness both

[1] M. Jahoda, "Consistency and Inconsistency in Intergroup Relations," *Journal of Social Issues*, 5, No. 3:4–12.

TABLE 14. PERCENTAGES OF HOUSEWIVES INDICATING (AS RATED BY INTERVIEWERS)
RESPECT FOR AND FRIENDLINESS TOWARD NEGRO PEOPLE

	Integrated Interracial Projects		Segregated Bi-Racial Projects	
	Koaltown (100)	Sacktown (89)	Bakerville (99)	Frankville (99)
Respect for				
Negro people in the project	51%	63%	24%	29%
Negro people in general	27	46	12	18
Friendliness toward				
Negro people in the project	30	50	9	6
Negro people in general	19	37	6	8

for the Negro people in the project and for the Negro people in general.[2] Table 14 summarizes data derived from these ratings.

It is clear from this table that the housewives in the integrated projects are more favorably disposed toward the Negro people in general, as well as toward the Negro people in their projects, than are the women in the segregated projects. This suggests that generalized changes in attitudes toward Negroes have taken place. However, if we contrast attitudes toward the Negro people in the project and attitudes toward the Negro in general, it is evident that changes in attitudes toward the Negro people in general were not as extensive as the changes in attitudes toward the Negro people in the project. That is, not all the housewives who changed their attitudes as a result of experiences with the Negro people in the project generalized their changes to include other Negro people.

In passing we should point out that the findings for the segregated projects support our suggestion in the previous chapter that more intimate experiences are necessary to effect a change in feelings than to bring about a change in beliefs. The lack of difference in the segregated projects between friendliness for the Negro people in the proj-

[2] In some respects, ratings by interviewers are superior to those obtained from the interview as recorded by the interviewer. The interviewer, in the situation, hearing and watching the housewife as she responds to questions designed to reveal her attitudes, has much more information upon which to base a judgment than the coder working from the written record of the interview. On the other hand, the judgments of interviewers frequently are unreliable because they are colored by irrelevancies (the housewife's appearance, her accent, etc.). Unless otherwise stated, as in this case, the information presented throughout this book is based upon the recorded interview rather than upon the interviewer's judgment. We found, however, that the judgments of the interviewers and the analysis of the recorded interviews give essentially the same results.

ect and for the Negro people in general probably indicates no change in feelings; on the other hand, the differences in the segregated projects between the percentage indicating respect for the Negro people in the project and the percentage indicating respect for the Negro people in general probably indicates some change in beliefs. This suggests that before a prejudiced person develops the desire to be friendly with Negro people he must first see them as "human beings" or equals. However, perceiving Negroes as equals provides only the opportunity for the development of friendly feelings; for this opportunity to be fully realized, intimate social contacts with Negroes on an equal-status basis seem to be necessary also.

REACTIONS TO STEREOTYPE QUESTIONS

During the course of the interview the housewives were asked to state whether they agreed with, were not sure about, or disagreed with the following statements: "Generally speaking, colored people are lazy and ignorant." "In general, colored people can't be trusted." And, "There's something different and strange about colored people; it's hard to tell what they're thinking and planning, or what makes them tick." The purpose of these questions was to provide us with additional information about the nature and frequency of the stereotypes of Negroes held by the housewife. Presenting the stereotypes in the affirmative, rather than in the negative (e.g., "Generally speaking, colored people are not any lazier or more ignorant than white people"), has the effect of making it less likely that the housewife will disagree. In a sense, by phrasing the statements as we did, we were putting a slight pressure on the housewife to agree with the stereotypes. Our justification for doing this is that typically in everyday life people encounter the stereotypes as we phrased them and it

TABLE 15. PERCENTAGES OF HOUSEWIVES DISAGREEING WITH INDICATED NUMBER OF STEREOTYPES

Response	Integrated Interracial Projects		Segregated Bi-Racial Projects	
	Koaltown (98)	Sacktown (89)	Bakerville (100)	Frankville (101)
Disagree with at least two stereotypes	50%	67%	33%	42%
Disagree with one of the three stereotypes	27	13	22	21
Disagree with none of the three stereotypes	23	20	45	37

seemed more instructive to get some notion of how the housewives would react when confronted with the statements in this form.

From Table 15, it is apparent that more housewives in Koaltown and Sacktown, as compared with those in Bakerville or Frankville, disagree with the stereotypes. In the former projects 50 percent and 67 percent, respectively, disagree with at least two of the stereotypes; in the latter projects, this is true of 33 percent of tenants in one case and 42 percent in the other. These differences may be taken as further evidence that the attitudes of many housewives in the integrated projects have changed not only toward the Negro people in the project but also toward the Negro people in general. However, the differences between the two types of projects are somewhat less in Table 15 than in the preceding tables, perhaps indicating that even under the slight pressure represented by the statement of the stereotype, people with attitudes like those of our integrated project housewives are less likely than otherwise to reject the prejudiced ideas circulating so freely in the broader community.

The most commonly accepted stereotype in all projects (see Table 16) is: "There's something different and strange about colored people; it's hard to tell what they're thinking and planning, or what makes them tick." Among the three stereotypes this one seems to represent a last stronghold for prejudiced beliefs retreating before conflicting experience. It is actually an unrationalized statement of difference; the apparent rationale comes from a "feeling," the existence of prejudiced sentiments. In effect, the individual is forced to use his feelings as a justification for his feelings. The greater retention of this stereotype suggests that in the attempt to develop wholesome intergroup attitudes, it is necessary not only to destroy the beliefs

TABLE 16. PERCENTAGES OF HOUSEWIVES DISAGREEING WITH
THREE STEREOTYPES ABOUT NEGROES

Stereotype	Integrated Interracial Projects		Segregated Bi-Racial Projects	
	Koaltown (98)	Sacktown (89)	Bakerville (100)	Frankville (101)
"Colored people are lazy and ignorant"	67%	74%	45%	54%
"Colored people can't be trusted"	52	67	38	46
"There's something different and strange about colored people"	33	56	16	32

TABLE 17. PERCENTAGES OF HOUSEWIVES IN DIFFERENT CLASSIFICATIONS
(OF POLITICAL ATTITUDES, EDUCATION, RELIGION) WHO REJECT AT
LEAST TWO OF THREE STEREOTYPES ABOUT NEGROES

	Integrated Interracial Projects		Segregated Bi-Racial Projects	
	Koaltown	Sacktown	Bakerville	Frankville
Political Attitudes				
Liberal	49% (35)*	77% (31)	50% (18)	49% (25)
Middle of the road ..	44 (32)	65 (23)	32 (37)	30 (37)
Conservative .	58 (31)	57 (35)	27 (45)	53 (38)
Education				
Only public school	37 (43)	46 (26)	18 (50)	31 (42)
Some high school	57 (28)	58 (31)	46 (33)	43 (35)
Completed high school or had some college .	80 (15)	87 (30)	50 (14)	79 (14)
Religion				
Protestant ...	50 (4)	75 (16)	31 (23)	25 (16)
Catholic	42 (17)	41 (39)	31 (66)	37 (40)
Jewish	50 (73)	96 (23)	43 (7)	52 (42)

* Figures in parentheses indicate the number of cases on which the percentage figures have been computed. In some cases, the numbers are so small as
to make the percentages relatively meaningless.

which support prejudices but also to stimulate actively the development of new positive feelings to replace the prejudiced feelings.

In all four of the projects, as may be seen from Table 17, there is
a marked relationship between lack of education and acceptance of
stereotypes about Negroes. Also, except in Koaltown, the Jewish
people accept significantly fewer stereotypes than either the Catholics
or the Protestants. These two facts help to explain why the differences between the housewives in Koaltown and Frankville (Table 15)
are relatively minor. Somewhat more than half of the Jewish women
in Koaltown have not gone to high school in this country; of this
group, slightly less than 30 percent disagree with at least two of the
stereotypes. In contrast, the Jewish women in Frankville are relatively well educated and assimilated; approximately two thirds have
gone to high school in this country. These population dissimilarities
tend to mask some of the differences in acceptance of stereotypes between Koaltown and Frankville which otherwise might appear as a
result of the occupancy pattern. Conversely, the difference between
Sacktown and Bakerville is enhanced by factors other than the occupancy pattern; there are both more Jewish people and more rela-

tively well-educated people who have completed high school in Sack-town than in Bakerville.

However, it is clear that when the influence of these factors is elim-inated, fewer housewives in the integrated projects stereotype the Negro people. Thus, if we compare Catholic housewives in both types of projects who are conservative in political outlook and who have only attended elementary school, we obtain the following results: 6 out of the *14* such housewives in the integrated projects disagree with at least two of the stereotypes; in the segregated projects, only *4* out of the *28* such housewives do likewise.

SOCIAL DISTANCE MEASURES[3]

Toward the end of every interview we presented the housewife with a list of groups of people (Chinese, Italian, Jewish, Negro, Puerto Rican, Irish, and English) and asked her to indicate which she would

TABLE 18. PERCENTAGES OF HOUSEWIVES RESPONDING NEGATIVELY TO THE IDEA OF HAVING NEGROES IN VARIOUS RELATIONSHIPS TO THEM*

Relationship	Integrated Interracial Projects		Segregated Bi-Racial Projects	
	Koaltown (97)	Sacktown (90)	Bakerville (100)	Frankville (96)
As mayor of the city	18%	19%	55%	31%
As tenants in the same building	25	22	82	72
As schoolmates of their children	33	31	59	51
As fellow members in an informal social club	43	26	83	63
As fellow workers	22	24	57	50

* It should be noted that few of the housewives who did *not* respond negatively indicated a desire to seek out these relationships with Negros. They are *neutral* rather than positive.

like to have and which she would not like to have as (1) officials of the city, (2) neighbors living in the same building, (3) pupils at-tending the same school as her children, (4) members of an informal social club, and (5) fellow employees on a job. Table 18 indicates the percentage of housewives who reacted negatively to the Negro

[3] We are presenting as many different lines of evidence as possible, in the belief that most attitudinal and behavioral measures available to the social scientist are only rough and unprecise indicators. Any single measure, by itself, should not in-spire much confidence. The accumulation of indicators which provide similar evi-dence establishes a basis for more confidence in research results.

group; reactions to other groups will be presented in a subsequent chapter.

The differences between the attitudes of the women in the two types of projects are marked. In the integrated projects less than one out of every four women indicate a desire not to live as neighbors to Negro families; a similar percentage do not wish to work with Negro people. In the segregated projects, over 70 percent dislike the thought of living next to Negro people and more than half would rather not work with them. Corresponding differences appear if we compare the reactions to having Negroes in the same social club or in the same school with the housewife's children, or to having one as mayor of the city.

It is interesting to note that the housewives in all four projects express the least resistance to the thought of having a Negro as mayor. This may be an expression of the democratic ethos which, perhaps, is seen by the housewife as being more directly applicable to political relations than to human relations. Or, it may be that politics is far removed from her main concerns and it makes little difference to her who is mayor. Apart from the reaction to the possibility of having a Negro mayor, the rank order for avoiding the various relationships differs, as one might expect, from the integrated to the segregated projects. In the segregated projects, the relationship which most housewives desire to avoid is that of "living in the same building." The housewives in the integrated projects, on the other hand, express relatively more opposition to "having children attend the same school with Negro children" and "having Negro women in a social club" than they do to "living in the same building."

These results clearly indicate substantial differences in attitudes between the housewives in the two types of projects toward Negro people in general. It seems reasonable to interpret these differences as being indicative of changes in attitudes among many of the women in the integrated projects. This change, as one would expect, most directly reflects itself in relation to feelings about "living in the same building with Negro people."

Attitude Changes as Reported by the Housewives

Perhaps the most striking data come from the reports of the housewives themselves about their own attitude changes toward Negroes in general. (Such reports must always be evaluated with caution because of distorting effects in recall. We have examined the data to see if differential distortion between the two types of projects might have occurred but could find no such indications.) We asked the housewives a series of questions which included the following: "Can you remember what you thought colored people were like before you moved into the project?" "How much have your ideas about colored people changed since you have lived in the project?" If some change, "In what ways have they changed?" and "What do you think made you change your ideas?"

TABLE 19. PERCENTAGES OF HOUSEWIVES IN THE PROJECT REPORTING FAVORABLE, NEUTRAL, OR UNFAVORABLE ATTITUDES TOWARD NEGROES PRIOR TO MOVING INTO IT

Prior Attitude	Integrated Interracial Projects		Segregated Bi-Racial Projects	
	Koaltown (99)	Sacktown (89)	Bakerville (99)	Frankville (100)
Favorable	15%	36%	13%	17%
Neutral	26	29	48	47
Unfavorable	59	35	39	36

Table 19 indicates the reported attitudes of the housewives before moving into their respective projects. The housewives in Sacktown report they were somewhat less prejudiced, while those in Koaltown report they were somewhat more prejudiced, than the housewives in the comparable segregated developments. A breakdown of Table 19 reveals that the differences between Sacktown and Koaltown arise largely from differences in the Jewish populations of the two projects. Thus 58 percent of the Jewish women in Koaltown as compared with 9 percent in Sacktown report they were originally unfavorable in attitudes toward the Negro people; 50 percent of the Jewish women in Sacktown report being originally favorable, and the corresponding figure for Koaltown is 15 percent. These differences between the Jewish women in the two projects are consistent with the data we have presented in earlier chapters and help to explain the findings of Table 19. It is interesting to note that if we compare our "standard group" in the two types of projects (the Catholic women who are politically conservative and who have had only an elementary school education) we obtain the following results: Out of the 14 such women in the integrated projects, 5 report having been originally unfavorable, 6 report having been neutral or ambivalent, and 3 report having been favorable. In the segregated projects the proportions are identical; 10 of the 28 such women indicate having been originally unfavorable, 12 report having been neutral, and 6 report having been favorable.[4]

[4] With such small numbers, of course, the exact correspondence of proportions should be considered a coincidence.

This striking correspondence may be taken as supporting our belief that no marked differential distortions occurred in the recall and in the reporting of attitudes by the housewives in the two types of projects.

TABLE 20. PERCENTAGES OF HOUSEWIVES IN THE PROJECT REPORTING FAVORABLE
CHANGE, NO CHANGE, OR UNFAVORABLE CHANGE IN THEIR
ATTITUDES TOWARD NEGROES

Present Attitude	Integrated Interracial Projects		Segregated Bi-Racial Projects	
	Koaltown (99)	Sacktown (89)	Bakerville (99)	Frankville (100)
Favorable change	59%	62%	27%	18%
No change	38	31	66	69
Unfavorable change	3	7	7	13

Table 20 reveals both the percentage of housewives who report changing their attitudes toward Negro people and the direction of change. The majority of housewives in the integrated projects report that they have become more favorable; only a few are less favorable. In the segregated projects there is also some increase in the number favorable, though the gain is to a greater extent offset by the housewives who have become less favorable. The *net gain* (percentage of housewives reporting favorable changes minus the percentage reporting unfavorable changes) is 56 percent and 55 percent for the integrated projects; for the segregated, it is 5 percent and 20 percent.

More detailed results, presented in Table 21, indicate that the *net gain* for the two integrated projects among housewives who report themselves as originally highly prejudiced is 71 percent and 78 percent; for the housewives originally moderately prejudiced, it is 46 percent and 61 percent; for housewives originally favorable it is 13 percent and 28 percent. In the two segregated projects, the corresponding net gains are much smaller: for those originally highly prejudiced it is 26 percent and 19 percent; for those originally moderately prejudiced, it is 18 percent and 2 percent; for those originally unprejudiced, there is a net gain of 15 percent in one and a *net loss* of 18 percent in the other segregated project.

It is clear from the above figures that, no matter what her original attitudes were, a housewife in the integrated project, if she changes them as a result of her experiences in the project, will most likely change them in a more favorable direction. Relatively, she is most likely to change, however, if her original attitudes were unfavorable

TABLE 21. PERCENTAGES OF HOUSEWIVES REPORTING CERTAIN PRESENT ATTITUDES
WHO WERE ORIGINALLY UNFAVORABLE, NEUTRAL, OR FAVORABLE TOWARD NEGROES

Present Attitude	Integrated Interracial Projects		Segregated Bi-Racial Projects	
	Koaltown (58)	Sacktown (31)	Bakerville (39)	Frankville (36)
Originally Unfavorable				
Favorable	50%	55%	8%	8%
More favorable, but not favorable	24	29	28	22
Still unfavorable (no change) .	23	10	54	59
Even more unfavorable	3	6	10	11
	Koaltown (26)	Sacktown (26)	Bakerville (47)	Frankville (47)
Originally Neutral, Indifferent, or Ambivalent				
Favorable	50%	69%	24%	13%
Still neutral (no change)	46	23	70	76
Unfavorable	4	8	6	11
	Koaltown (15)	Sacktown (32)	Bakerville (13)	Frankville (17)
Originally Favorable				
Even more favorable	13%	34%	15%	6%
Still favorable (no change) ..	87	60	85	70
Less favorable	0	6	0	6
Unfavorable	0	0	0	18

and least likely to change (as would be expected) if her original attitudes were favorable. In the segregated projects, if the housewife's original attitudes were unfavorable or neutral, any attitude change is also more likely than not to be reported in a favorable direction. This cannot be asserted unequivocally for those in the latter type project who were originally favorably disposed toward Negroes.

The interview material provides dramatic illustration of the nature of the attitudinal changes which occurred among many of the housewives in the integrated projects. Thus, one woman when asked to tell how she felt about living in the project, said, "I started to cry when my husband told me we were coming to live here. I cried for three weeks. I didn't want to come and live here where there were so many colored people. I didn't want to bring my children up with colored children, but we had to come; there was no place else to go. Well, all that's changed. I've really come to like it. I see they're just as human as we are. They have nice apartments, they keep their children clean, and they're friendly. I've come to like them a great deal. I'm no longer scared of them. I'd just as soon live near a colored person as a white; it makes no difference to me." Another women put it quaintly: "I thought I was moving into the heart of Africa. I had always heard things about how they were . . . they were dirty, drink a lot . . . were like savages. Living with them, my ideas have changed altogether. They're just people. They're not any different." Another one said: "I was prejudiced when I moved in here but not any more. . . . I find there is no such thing as 'my kind.' I was under the impression that every colored man that looked at you wanted to rape you or was going to pull out a razor. I don't feel that way any more. I know the people, I have been in their home . . . been to church with them. I know they're not dirty. My doctor is colored. My dentist is colored. He's a surgeon and he's wonderful."

In contrast to the above, the following remarks express typical findings in the segregated projects: "I don't have anything to do with the colored people . . . they don't bother me . . . I don't mingle with them. I guess I don't like them because they're colored. The Bible says, 'God created them equal,' so I guess they're equal, but I don't like them. I don't like living so close to them. I think they ought to be in separate projects. Let them live their lives and let us live ours. . . . My ideas haven't changed any since I've lived here. They're colored and I'm white. They don't like us and we don't like them."

While the above quotations from the integrated project report striking changes, they are not atypical of the people who originally had unfavorable attitudes but changed to favorable attitudes. In all of them, the same pattern is repeated: little experience with Negroes before moving into the project and strong stereotypes (they're murderous, dirty, drunk, savage, uncivilized, etc.) accepted from those circulating in the culture at large, experiences with Negroes in the project in the course of close neighborly associations who differ strikingly from the stereotypes, and the gradual development of more friendly attitudes growing out of these experiences.

The few instances of changes in an unfavorable direction in the integrated projects follow a different pattern. For example, one woman in Sacktown, who became more unfavorable, said, "I figured they were human beings like we were . . . at first I thought they wanted to get along with other people but they seem to have a chip on their shoulder . . . they let you know that they don't like your living with them. They're very spiteful . . . and the dirty looks you get. They act as though *you* should be the humbler . . . they say you're 'white trash' to your face. . . . My small daughter got beaten up and if

you say anything . . . the mothers come out and start arguing. . . .
You can't win with them." The complaint of another housewife who
changed in an unfavorable direction was similar: "They think they're
better than we are." These housewives may have carried with them
without realizing it the expectations of the dominant white as they
moved into a community where the Negro people are in the majority.
The Negro people in the project sensitive to prejudiced attitudes
and free to express their resentment have, perhaps, openly challenged
these expectations, to the embarrassment and discomfort of these
housewives.

Some of the women who changed in an unfavorable direction state
specific unpleasant experiences. "I left my baby downstairs in the
carriage, while I went up for something. When I came down I couldn't
find my baby. I looked everywhere. I was nearly crazy for four hours
. . . until I finally found my baby in a garbage can. It was some of
the colored kids who did it, I found out later." A number of the
women, particularly in Frankville, report unpleasant experiences with
Negro people in the neighborhood around the project: "They're drunk
and they follow you at night. I was walking down the street and
one of them followed me for two blocks, making remarks. . . . I
won't go out alone when it is dark now." [5]

THE PEOPLE WHO CHANGE

Many housewives in the integrated projects and some in the segregated projects have reported change to more favorable attitudes toward Negroes while others have indicated no change. Why did some
housewives change and others not? Are there any clearly identifiable
characteristics which make one housewife more likely to change attitudes than another? To provide a satisfactory answer to this question, it would have been necessary to study many more people than
it was possible for us to do. Nevertheless, our material provides some
tentative answers. We offer our suggestions without any statistical
elaboration because the number of cases on which they are based are,
for the most part, very small.

If we compare, in the integrated projects, the housewives who
have reported changing to a more favorable attitude toward Negroes
with the housewives who have not reported changing (both types

[5] In all the projects, we suspect that one of the main factors limiting the generalization of the favorable experiences with Negroes-in-the-project to Negroes-in-general
was their location. The projects were located in deteriorated, delinquent Negro neighborhoods. The experiences in the neighborhood, the association of "deterioration" and
"delinquency" with "Negro" may well have limited the effects of the experiences in
the project.

of housewives reporting unfavorable or neutral attitudes prior to moving into the projects), we obtain the following conclusions:

1. The people who report no change have had relatively fewer intimate contacts with Negroes; proportionately fewer of them indicate a Negro as one of the persons they know best in the project; considerably more of them state that they have no neighborly activities in common with Negro women; comparatively fewer have had, prior to moving into the project, equal-status contact experiences with Negroes.

2. The people who report change are relatively more cohesive members of the project community than those who do not. They like the people in the project relatively more; they know more people in the project, are more likely to belong to an organization within the project, and are more likely to engage in neighborly activities with other women in the project.

3. The people who change are more likely to report that their friends expect them to be friendly with the Negro people.

4. The people who report no change are more likely to have low morale. They are more likely to dislike living in the project and to indicate distress or unhappiness in answer to the question, "Generally speaking, how happy are you with your present state of affairs?"

5. There seems to be no clear-cut relation between reported change and political attitudes or religion (except that those who indicate regular religious observance are less likely to report change than those who are less regular in observance). However, housewives who are younger, housewives who identify themselves as "working class" rather than "middle class," and those who have had at least a high school education are more likely to report change than elderly women or those who have had only an elementary school education.

6. And, as one would expect if our data are at all self-consistent, the housewives who report change are less prejudiced and favor interracial housing more than do the women who do not change.

Any attempt at an explanation of the above results runs into the age-old problem of the chicken and the egg. Which comes first? Is it the predisposition to change which results in more contact with Negroes, or is it the contact which causes the change? Does low morale make it less likely that a person will be friendly with his Negro neighbors, or does having Negro neighbors make for low morale? We cannot provide any conclusive answer to these questions with the data available from a study of this type.

However, it may be of interest to attempt a composite characterization of the people who changed to more favorable attitudes, as compared with those who did not: When they moved into the project, though typically prejudiced, they were relatively young and comparatively better educated. As a consequence of casual experiences at school or in factories during the war Negroes were not completely strange to them. Placed in a situation where contact with Negroes was almost inevitable, they had more flexibility and experience with which to make an adaptation. To live with Negroes as next-door neighbors presented, furthermore, less of a status threat because they pictured themselves as being "working class" rather than "middle class." Adapting themselves to their Negro neighbors instead of withdrawing and cutting themselves off brought closer contact with Negroes, and with closer contact many prejudices were shed. As a consequence of their friendly relations with the Negro people, they faced many problems in relation to the prejudiced broader community. Sharing these problems with their white neighbors, they were drawn closer to them and came to know them and like them better than did the women who had cut themselves off from relations with the Negro people. As a consequence of this closer bond with other members of the project community, they were more aware of and exposed to the social norms regarding race relations that characterized the project community. Their social life in the project was generally satisfactory, and they enjoyed living in it

In contrast, the housewives who (because of age, lack of education, or middle-class identification) lacked the flexibility to adapt to intimate social contacts with Negroes were relatively uncomfortable in the integrated projects. By cutting themselves off from the Negro people, they were led also to limit their social relations with the other white people in the project in order to avoid embarrassing situations and the social pressures toward conformity to the social norms of the project. As a result, the ratios of their outside friends to friends within the project were higher than those of the housewives who changed in attitudes.

While the above descriptions of the housewives who changed and of the housewives who did not change seem to us to be plausible, it should be noted again that they are constructed from a small number of cases. The process of change is more safely inferred from a longitudinal study over a period of time of people as they move in and live in projects than from a cross-sectional study such as ours.[6]

---

[6] We have analyzed our data in terms of the length of residence of the housewife. This analysis, unfortunately, runs into several obstacles. For example, in Koaltown only a small percentage has lived in the project for less than two years, while in Sacktown, though there is a relatively high percentage of move-ins since the war, the latter are not directly comparable with those who have been living in the project for

In summary, we have presented a variety of evidence which is pertinent to the question of whether or not the experiences of living in an integrated interracial project produce, in addition to changes of attitudes toward the Negro people in the project, more favorable attitudes toward Negro people in general. The ratings made by our interviewers, the responses of the housewives to "stereotype" and "social distance" questions, and the reports from the housewives about their own attitude changes all lead to the same answer: Considerable generalized changes in attitudes toward Negroes have occurred among the people living in the integrated projects. It is clear, on the other hand, that not all housewives who have come to respect and like their Negro neighbors extend their feelings to Negro people in general. From data to be reported in Chapter XI it seems likely that an important factor limiting the generalization of attitudinal change is the location of the projects in deteriorated, delinquent neighborhoods which also happen to be predominantly Negro.

The reports of the housewives indicate that approximately 60 percent of the white women in the integrated projects have become less prejudiced and that only about 5 percent have become more prejudiced. In contrast about 75 percent of the women in the segregated projects indicate no reduction in prejudice; of these approximately 10 percent report becoming more prejudiced. We have presented a comparison of the housewives who report favorable change with the housewives who do not. While the comparison is based on a relatively small number of cases, results are consistent with our other results and suggestive for further research.

a number of years. The people who have moved in since the war have moved in, by and large, as a result of veterans' preference; they are younger, better educated, less prejudiced, more liberal, etc. than the older, more typical residents in low-rent public housing projects.

In both Koaltown and Sacktown there is a tendency for the housewives with longer lengths of residence to know more people, Negro and white, in the project. In Koaltown this tendency is associated with less prejudice; in Sacktown, however, owing to the fact that the newer tenants were younger and initially relatively unprejudiced, this relationship between length of residence and lack of prejudice is not found. In the segregated bi-racial projects, the women with longer lengths of residence tend to report a greater likelihood of "getting to know" Negro people in the project; there is, however, no clear relationship, in these projects, between lack of prejudice and length of residence.

CHAPTER X

Attitudes toward Other Minority Groups

MANY studies of prejudice have revealed a close relationship between attitudes toward one minority group and attitudes toward other minority groups. A person who is biased against Negroes is likely to be hostile toward the Chinese, and, contrariwise, the individual who is relatively free of prejudice toward any minority group (against whom there is considerable prejudice in the community) is likely to be free of bigotry toward other minorities. Few studies, however, have been made which indicate the effects of change in attitudes toward one group upon attitudes toward another.

Such studies would be of considerable significance to theories of prejudice. They might help to clarify the question of whether or not prejudice toward any group usually reflects deep personality needs or whether it is usually a mirror of social traditions which tend to perpetuate themselves by the practices, beliefs, and values to which they give rise.[1] If it is primarily a function of deep personality needs, reduction in prejudice toward any one group could not be expected without either a change in basic personality (with the probable consequence of a general reduction of prejudice) or without resulting in a compensating increase in prejudice toward other groups. On the other hand, if prejudice principally reflects social traditions, then a change in practices and prejudice toward one group may not affect prejudices toward other groups except (1) when the social traditions apply in an undifferentiated fashion to various minority groups, e.g., to "all foreigners" or to "all people with dark skin," or (2) when the

[1] There is, of course, no necessary antithesis between the "personality" and the "social" approach to prejudice. Most social scientists would probably agree that both personality and social traditions are operative in the development of prejudice: personality determining the relative degree of prejudice the various individuals in a social group will have, and the social traditions determining the level of prejudice around which the individuals will vary as well as the range of variations.

beliefs and values which develop to support prejudiced social practices toward various minority groups are similar, or (3) when special
educational efforts are made to generalize experiences with one minority group to that of another.

In the course of our interviewing, we collected some information
about the housewives' attitudes toward the Chinese and Puerto Rican
groups (among others). We were particularly interested in these
two groups because, like the Negro group, they are objects of prejudice and, in addition, neither is represented in the projects to any
extent (less than 1 percent of the residents in any of the projects are
Puerto Rican or Chinese). Clearly, if the attitudes of the housewives
changed toward the Chinese or Puerto Rican, it would not have been
a result of their experiences with them in the project; more likely,
it would have reflected alterations in attitudes toward the Negroes.
Such generalization, if it occurred, would not, however, be a consequence of special educational efforts to produce it, since in none
of the projects was there such an effort.

The information we obtained about attitudes toward Puerto Ricans
and Chinese was acquired through questions of the "social distance"
type. These data are summarized in Table 22. Though the differences
are smaller than in preceding tables, the housewives in the integrated
projects are relatively less unfavorable toward the Chinese than are
the women in Bakerville or Frankville. The largest difference between
the two types of projects occurs, as one would expect, in relation to
"living in the same building," this being opposed by 40 percent and
23 percent in Koaltown and Sacktown as against 60 percent and 52
percent in Bakerville and Frankville. The attitudes of the housewives
toward Puerto Ricans in the two types of projects are on the whole
quite similar.

Let us consider the implications of these results for the theory
which stresses that prejudice is primarily a function of deep personality needs. The implications of this theory, it will be remembered,
lead us to expect that a reduction in prejudice toward one minority
group should be accompanied either by an increase in prejudice toward another group or by a basic change in personality. The first of
these two alternatives is, of course, at variance with our results. We
find associated with a reduction in prejudice toward Negroes a parallel though less frequent reduction in prejudice toward the Chinese —
rather than, as the theory implies, a compensating increase.

However, the second of the alternative implications, that of an
associated basic change in personality, could be regarded as consistent with our findings. The argument requires that the percentages

TABLE 22. PERCENTAGES OF HOUSEWIVES RESPONDING NEGATIVELY TO THE IDEA OF
HAVING NEGROES, CHINESE, OR PUERTO RICANS IN VARIOUS
RELATIONSHIPS TO THEM

	Integrated Interracial Projects		Segregated Bi-Racial Projects	
	Koaltown (97)	Sacktown (90)	Bakerville (100)	Frankville (96)
As Mayor of the City				
Negro	18%	19%	55%	31%
Chinese	24	31	44	34
Puerto Rican	15	23	32	19
As Tenants in the Same Building				
Negroes	25	22	82	72
Chinese	40	23	60	52
Puerto Ricans	32	28	40	30
As Schoolmates of Their Children				
Negroes	33	31	59	51
Chinese	22	23	37	26
Puerto Ricans	19	21	28	19
As Fellow Club Members				
Negroes	43	26	83	63
Chinese	34	29	45	35
Puerto Ricans	21	23	26	23
As Fellow Workers				
Negroes	22	24	57	50
Chinese	22	20	42	28
Puerto Ricans	16	18	21	13
In Any Relationship				
Negroes	42	36	88	75
Chinese	53	44	73	55
Puerto Ricans	42	41	61	40

for the segregated bi-racial projects in Table 22 be interpreted to mean that the pre-project attitudes of many tenants in each of the four projects were originally less prejudiced toward Chinese than toward Negroes and that even more were less prejudiced toward Puerto Ricans. In turn, the percentages for the integrated projects, although they show considerable variation from item to item, can be interpreted to mean that approximately three quarters of these tenants hold relatively little prejudice against any one of the three groups. The remaining quarter of the integrated tenants must be assumed, in this argument, to have held, initially, relatively high prejudice against all three groups and to have retained these attitudes through the point at which our interviews were made. These latter tenants, it would be argued, underwent no personality change and remained prejudiced. Some portion of the former three quarters did change in personality structure and lost such prejudice as they had.

The reason for observing among these tenants more frequent change toward Negroes than toward Chinese and Puerto Ricans is that more of them held initial anti-Negro attitudes.

However, sound this argument may be, it rests on an assumption that changes in basic personality did occur in a large number of our subjects as a consequence of their experiences in interracial housing projects. This appears quite unlikely in view of what is generally believed about the difficulty of making changes in character structure. One investigator has described the difficulty of modifying the prejudiced personality as follows: "His personality structure is highly resistant to change in any of the dimensions enumerated. His response to psychiatric therapy or guidance would be poor. His problems are deep-seated and not amenable to alteration without a fundamental change in his entire style of life. Because of the unavoidable inconsistencies between life's demands and the systems of defenses and subterfuges which he has built up, he is chronically maladjusted in the psychiatric sense." [2]

It would be instructive in future research to check the "personality theory" of prejudice by seeing whether a change in attitudes toward a minority group is accompanied by a change in such factors as attitudes toward authority and sex, rigidity of thinking, and ego-strength. If this theory is correct, a major reduction in prejudice should be accompanied by changes in these factors.

As noted at the beginning of the chapter, an alternative to the theory that basic personality structure is the major determinant of prejudice is the belief that prejudices reflect social traditions and social practices which have been accepted and internalized. To the extent that the individual has been exposed to similar traditions of prejudice in relation to various groups, his prejudices toward these groups are likely to be similar; to the extent that the traditions he has been exposed to are different his attitudes toward the various minority groups are likely to be dissimilar.

One reason for the commonly found relationship, in correlational studies, among attitudes toward various groups may be the similarity of many of the social traditions toward the various minority groups. Prejudices toward different minority groups frequently serve analogous social and economic purposes. This parallelism of social functions may give rise to a similarity in social attitudes within the individual without necessarily creating a functional interdependence

[2] H. G. Gough, "Personality Correlates of Social and Ethnic Attitudes Among High School Students," unpublished Ph.D. thesis, University of Minnesota, March 1949.

among the attitudes or without resulting in their being functionally dependent, in common, upon more basic personality structures. That is, the correlation among attitudes toward various minority groups, according to this theory, primarily reflects a *social* or external, rather than a *personality* or internal, relationship. Of course, under certain circumstances (particularly of close similarity among the minority groups or of close similarity in the social practices of the majority groups toward the minority groups), the external relationship may generate an internal relationship so that the attitudes become functionally interdependent for the individual. To be sure, our data suggest some functional relationship between attitudes toward Negroes and attitudes toward the Chinese. We have not sufficient information to tell whether this relationship arises through both being in the category of "colored" races or through their both being relatively low-status groups, or whether, as we have indicated above, it points to their both being dependent upon more basic personality structures.

Table 22 summarizes in another way the "social distance" attitudes we have been discussing and throws a somewhat different light upon their interpretation. In this table we have grouped all tenants who reject any one or more of the five types of association with each of the three ethnic groups. By subtraction it is possible, of course, to indicate the proportion of tenants who reject *none* of the social relationships, i.e., who insofar as these five items are concerned are entirely unprejudiced. The figures for the segregated project are consistent with what general observation would lead one to expect for the cities studied: in the case of the Chinese a somewhat greater proportion of the tenants accept all the social relationships mentioned than is true in the case of the Negroes. However, for the integrated projects this order is reversed. In Koaltown 58 percent accept all the relationships with the Negro group against 47 percent who accept all for the Chinese. In Sacktown the corresponding figures are 64 percent against 56 percent. In other words, a number of tenants in the integrated projects who have become by this criterion "entirely unprejudiced" against Negroes retain some prejudice against the Chinese (it is well to recall that we are making the assumption that pre-project attitudes were similar in the integrated and segregated projects). For these tenants at least there would appear to be no necessary functional interdependence in attitudes toward different minority groups.

To sum up, while the data presented in this chapter are meager, they suggest that reduction in prejudice toward the Negroes among the integrated housewives has brought with it some change in attitudes toward the Chinese. They suggest also that the high correlations commonly found among attitudes toward various minority groups do not necessarily indicate a close functional interdependence of the attitudes that are highly correlated: a change in one may not result in a change in the other. Nevertheless, there appears to be some functional relationship between attitudes toward Negroes and attitudes toward the Chinese among the housewives we studied.

CHAPTER XI

Attitudes toward Living in an Interracial Project

THERE are many factors which play a role in determining whether an individual will like or dislike the place in which he lives. Our research interest, however, was not primarily oriented toward finding out the satisfactions and dissatisfactions of the housewife with the housing project as a place in which to live. Rather it was directed toward discovering her attitudes toward its interracial character and how these attitudes had been shaped by her experiences with interracial housing. Yet, as the comparison of the people who became less prejudiced with the people who didn't revealed (see Chapter IX), the two are not unrelated. Since the average housewife in the integrated project, as a result of her neighborly contacts with members of the other race, has become less prejudiced, one would expect her to be more hospitable to the idea of interracial housing than her counterpart in the segregated project. Conversely, as a consequence of her relatively greater dislike of interracial housing one would expect the housewife in the segregated project to be less happy living in a project which has interracial characteristics.

While, as we have indicated above, it is to be expected that there will be a positive relationship between attitudes toward Negroes and attitudes toward living in an interracial project, it cannot be assumed that this relationship will be a perfect one. Many other factors may influence one's attitude toward an interracial project, such as the nature of the neighborhood, the attitude of friends, one's aspirations for one's children.

THE HOUSEWIFE'S REACTION TO LIVING IN AN INTERRACIAL PROJECT

To obtain the housewife's reaction to living in an interracial project we asked her, "How do you feel about living in a project where there

110

are colored and white families?" While the words are the same, it must be understood that this question has different implications for the housewives in the two types of projects. For the housewives in the integrated projects, it has the implied additional phrase, "in the same building"; in the segregated projects, the implication is, "in the project but in different buildings." That is, the question asks about a more intense relationship in the integrated projects.

Even so, the majority (67 percent in Koaltown and 71 percent in Sacktown) of the women have positive feelings toward the interracial aspects of their projects. In contrast, many housewives in the segregated projects (in Bakerville 54 percent and in Frankville 36 percent) react as though they were not living in an interracial project because they have so little contact with Negro tenants. Of the women in the segregated projects who do acknowledge the interracial composition, slightly more than half respond negatively. In the integrated projects, the ratio of housewives who indicate that they have come to like living in an interracial project more rather than less since first moving into their projects is more than three to one; in contrast, of the housewives in Bakerville and Frankville the ratio of those who like it less rather than more is two to one.

Such reactions as the following to the interracial characteristics of the project are not atypical for the housewives in Sacktown and Koaltown: "I think it's a wonderful idea. It helps you to get to know different kinds of people." "It's an excellent lesson in democracy." "It's a good idea, it breaks down barriers." In Bakerville and Frankville, on the other hand, many housewives say: "We have nothing to do with each other. We stay on our side and they stay on their side." Or, "They're way over there."

When asked to tell us what they disliked about living in a project which contained Negro and white families, the housewives in all projects reveal that one of the most important reasons for disliking the projects is the neighborhoods in which they are located. Partly their objection is to the neighborhood being Negro and partly their experience leads them to believe that living in an interracial project means living in a delinquency-ridden, deteriorated neighborhood. Some housewives object to the fact that their children go to school with Negroes; some state that they are afraid to walk home from the subways alone, or that their friends won't come to visit them if they have to walk through the neighborhood at night.

It is interesting to note that in the segregated projects a statement such as "I don't go out at night because I am afraid to walk in this neighborhood when it is dark" frequently occurs in the context of statements about Negroes. In the integrated projects, while similar statements are made, they rarely imply a derogatory comment about Negroes; the statement is about a deteriorated neighborhood which also happens to be Negro. Thus, when talking adversely about the project neighborhoods, more than half of the housewives in the segregated projects describe it as a Negro neighborhood rather than as a low-class or slum neighborhood; in contrast, more than three times as many women in the integrated projects when depicting the negative aspects of their neighborhood use words like "slum," "delinquent," or "low-class" rather than words like "Negro" or "colored." We may speculate that a consequence of living as neighbors with Negro people is that when one encounters a situation which includes the three elements, slums, Negroes, and delinquency, the tendency will be more frequently to link delinquency with slums and less frequently with Negroes.

When asked to tell us what they liked about living in a project which contained both Negro and white families, of the housewives in all of the projects who indicated specific factors liked, most pointed out that they like the fact that it's democratic. One woman in Koaltown said, "Everybody should be equal; so far as I am concerned there's no difference to me whether the people here are Negro or white." Another stated, "You get to know all types. It makes people more tolerant."

THE PROJECT AS A PLACE FOR CHILDREN

As part of a series of queries, in which the housewife was asked to imagine she was being questioned about the project by a friend who knew nothing about it, we asked the following: "You know I have two children . . . my girl is fourteen and my boy is nine. What would it mean for them to live in a project where there are colored and white families?" We were, of course, interested in obtaining information about the views of the housewife on the effects upon children of the project in which she lived.

The views of the women in the two types of projects are somewhat different. A sizable minority of the housewives in the segregated projects (32 percent in Bakerville and 15 percent in Frankville) say, "The colored kids and the white kids don't have much to do with each other. White kids stay on their side, colored kids on their side." None of the women in the integrated projects make such statements. Of those who assert definite opinions, pro or con, about the effects of the racial composition of the project upon the children, in each of the integrated projects 56 percent make positive and 44 percent make negative statements; in Bakerville 46 percent and in Frankville 51 percent make positive statements.

While the percentages of women in the two types of projects who make positive statements about life for children in the project are similar, relatively more housewives in the integrated projects point out (in the words of a mother in Sacktown): "This has been a wonderful experience for my children. They have had an opportunity to learn to be unprejudiced."

The negative evaluations of the women in Bakerville and Frankville most commonly expressed themselves as a feeling that "children should be brought up with their own kind." This was also a frequently offered reaction in the integrated projects. The most common negative reaction, however, in the integrated projects was to the neighborhood and to the schools in the neighborhood. Thus, one Koaltown housewife said, "The schools around here are awful. They're 90 percent colored. There aren't enough teachers. I don't think they keep up the schools in colored sections too well. The good teachers won't come here. I want to move to ——— where I can send my boy to a better school."

It's interesting to note that though we included in our question about children a reference to a fourteen-year-old girl so as to stimulate responses indicating anxieties or problems in relation to the adolescent girl in a racially mixed project, we obtained relatively few answers which would indicate that intermarriage, as such, is a source of concern. Only 1 percent of the women in each of the two segregated projects, 5 percent in Koaltown, and 12 percent in Sacktown indicate that white girls have specific problems. These women, for the most part, indicate that the white girls are socially handicapped by the fact that there aren't so many white boys of an adolescent age as there might be in an all-white neighborhood. The fear of intermarriage expressed in the following quotations from an interview with a woman in Sacktown is a worry to only a few housewives; to these few, it is, however, a major source of anxiety: "I want my children to grow up to be unprejudiced — yet I am worried about Ann, my daughter. She's grown up so that she doesn't see any differences between Negro and white people. She's only twelve now . . . there are a lot of fine Negro boys here in the project . . . she's likely to just naturally fall in love with one. If she does, it would be such a mess — people are so prejudiced — she'd never be happy. I don't know what to do. It would be all right, I guess, if everybody weren't so prejudiced against mixed marriages. . . . I've been thinking a lot about it lately and worrying. I'll probably move out before Ann gets much older."

In their evaluations of the desirability of the projects for children, the differences between the white housewives in the two types of projects are not marked, but this is what one might expect. The children, for each of the housewives, carry with them her status aspirations for the future; in them she has placed many of her major hopes and ambitions. The prejudice of the broader community is such as to place social censure upon those who freely associate with Negroes; one runs less of a social risk if one's children are brought up with children of "one's own kind."

The Negro housewife, having generally less status in the eyes of the broader community than her white counterpart, is in a somewhat different position and one would expect different responses. *All* of the 45 Negro housewives interviewed in the integrated projects who express unambiguous opinions express positive feelings about the project for their children. They make such statements as these: "It's a distinct advantage. The children will grow up without an inferiority complex." "They'll learn that there's no difference between them and the whites." "They'll find out in practice something about those theories [i.e., with respect to democracy] they've been hearing about in school." None indicate a fear of intermarriage or a feeling that their children might be emotionally hurt by the white children. In contrast, 34 of the 50 Negro women interviewed in Bakerville and Frankville state that the Negro and white children have nothing to do with one another in the project;[1] the remaining 16 feel that the children will get along well together. A number of the Negro women in the segregated projects, particularly in Bakerville, who indicate that the children of the two races don't play together express resentment at this fact. A reaction such as the following was not atypical: "The project keeps the children apart; they ought to do away with segregation. It would do the children good to mix."

The interviews with the children in Bakerville and Sacktown directly reveal how the children themselves feel about living in their respective projects. Fifteen of the 24 children questioned in Sacktown expressed enthusiasm for living in the project, describing it as "nice" or "fine," or saying, "It's fun to live here"; 6 described it as "okay" or "all right" and 3 indicated that they did not like it. Two of these

[1] In Frankville, where there is only one playground for use by the children in the project, there is evidently considerably more interaction among the Negro and white children than in Bakerville where there are play areas on both sides of the project. Thus 50 percent of the Negro women in Frankville and only 12 percent in Bakerville indicate positive relations between the children of the two races.

three children stated they didn't like to live among colored people. One of these two had been living in Sacktown only four months and had no friends, white or Negro; the other indicated that her parents felt the same way.

In contrast to Sacktown, in Bakerville 20 of the 24 children were unenthusiastic about living there. Most of the white children among the 20 complained that they used to have a large playground on their side of the project which had been taken away from them. They expressed considerable feeling about this because the Negro children still had their playground on their side. Some expressed resentment because they were not permitted to form a club on the project unless the Negro children were allowed to join. The Negro children, while for the most part not directly criticizing the occupancy pattern, also were unenthusiastic about living in the project. They too expressed a sense of rivalry with the white children for the facilities and for the manager's approval.

Thus, while many other factors are undoubtedly also operating, it seems probable that the segregation of races (with the resulting competition for facilities) has made the children in Bakerville relatively less enthusiastic about their project than are the unsegregated children of Sacktown. It is also evident that the children in Sacktown are considerably more favorable toward their project than are their mothers. Many of the white mothers, with aspirations for their children oriented toward the future, are apprehensive about their children's close relationships with Negro children (though they do not necessarily disapprove or discourage it); their children, as yet unconcerned with and unencumbered by the prejudices of the broader community, enjoy the community in which they live.

PREFERENCES WITH RESPECT TO THE OCCUPANCY PATTERN

The women in the projects are citizens in a democracy and as citizens they may have influence in shaping public policy. To ascertain the effects of their experiences in their respective projects in determining their views on policy with respect to interracial housing, we asked the following question: "On the basis of your experience of living in a project where there are colored and white families, what plan do you think the city should follow in new projects? Do you think that colored and white families should be given apartments anywhere in the project, no matter what their race is, *or* do you think colored and white families should be allowed to live only in separate buildings in the project, *or* do you think projects should be only all-white or all-colored?" The responses are summarized in Table 23.

TABLE 23. PERCENTAGES OF HOUSEWIVES RECOMMENDING A CITY POLICY IN NEW
PROJECTS OF ASSIGNING NEGRO AND WHITE FAMILIES TO ANY PLACE
IN ANY PROJECT, TO SEPARATE BUILDINGS IN ONE PROJECT, OR TO
SEPARATE PROJECTS

Assignment Recommended	Integrated Interracial Projects		Segregated Bi-Racial Projects	
	Koaltown (96)	Sacktown (88)	Bakerville (100)	Frankville (96)
To any place in any project	53%	53%	4%	6%
To separate buildings in one project	9	7	23	25
To separate projects	38	40	73	69

The opinions of the housewives in the integrated projects are in sharp contrast to those of the women in the segregated projects. The majority of respondents in the former favor the integrated pattern; the housewives in the latter, on the other hand, would overwhelmingly prefer to have completely separate projects for Negro and white families. Of considerable interest is the fact that among the housewives in the integrated projects there are a number who feel satisfied with living in an integrated interracial project but who would not recommend it as a policy for their city to follow in new projects. This is clear from the fact that only 53 percent recommended such a policy in contrast to the 67 percent in Koaltown and the 71 percent in Sacktown who had expressed positive feelings toward the interracial character of the project in which they lived.

One gets the impression from the interviews that a number of people who are positive in their attitudes toward living in an integrated interracial project find it a strain to buck the prejudices of the larger community. Others, who would just as soon have Negroes as neighbors, feel that many other white people are prejudiced and that these people might cause trouble.

The reactions of the Negro housewives to the same question are rather different. In the integrated projects, 47 of the 49 Negro women interviewed state their preference for the integrated pattern; the other two would prefer projects which are all-white or all-Negro because they feel the white people would rather have it that way. The majority of the Negro women in the segregated projects (30 out of 50) also favor the integrated; 13 of 50 prefer the bi-racial pattern; the remainder would rather have all-white or all-Negro projects. Most of the Negro women believe that separation of the two races is, in effect, discrimination and feel that the separation implies Negro inferiority. Hence naturally they reject the notion of any form of separation and welcome the thought of changing the attitudes of white people. Thus one Negro woman in Koaltown stated, "Separate buildings or separate projects would be segregation and that's what we're trying to fight. When you live together and some whites who want to segregate see that others are getting along all right, they change and at least begin to act friendly whether they really like Negroes or not." A woman in Bakerville expressed her feelings more resentfully: "There's no difference in us. Our money is just as good as theirs."

The Negro women in Bakerville and Frankville who favor separate projects or separate buildings do so largely as a defense against prejudice. Such statements as the following are given as reasons for their preference: "They are so prejudiced; I'd be afraid to live among them." Some of the Negro women in the segregated projects also appear to have absorbed the prejudices of the whites toward their group and react with a feeling of racial inferiority: "Negroes sometimes are abusive and don't take care of projects . . . wouldn't be good neighbors." This "self-hatred" which is to be found among some members of all minority groups is one of the most debasing consequences of prejudice.[2]

The children in the two projects were also questioned about their preferences in relation to the occupancy pattern. Twenty-one of the 24 children in Sacktown stated they liked it the way it is . . . unsegregated. Thirteen of the 24 children in Bakerville also stated their approval of the status quo, 5 white children indicated a preference for an all-white project (none of the Negro children preferred an all-Negro project), 3 children did not indicate a preference, and 3 Negro children thought that the Negro and white families should live more closely together. Clearly, the patterns they find existing at hand play a large role in determining the children's preferences about the occupancy pattern.

THE EFFECTS OF THE OCCUPANCY PATTERN VERSUS THE EFFECTS OF RELIGION, EDUCATION, AND POLITICAL ATTITUDES

In several previous chapters, we have stressed the necessity of considering the possibility that the dissimilarities between the two types of projects revealed by our data might be adequately explained by differences in religion, education, and/or political attitudes. Let us consider, for illustrative purposes, the responses of the housewives to our question about occupancy pattern policy. We may subdivide Table 23 so that we compare only women of the same religion, of similar

[2] K. Lewin, *Resolving Social Conflicts* (Harper, 1948).

education, or of similar political attitudes. Such an analysis (see Table 24) reveals that it makes relatively little difference whether the housewife is educated or not, liberal or conservative, Jewish or Catholic; if she lives in a segregated bi-racial project, she is not likely to recommend a policy of integration. On the other hand, even if her predispositions as a result of education, religion, and political attitudes are unfavorable, if she lives in an integrated project she is more likely to recommend an integrated policy than if she is favorably predisposed and is living in a segregated project.

TABLE 24. PERCENTAGES OF HOUSEWIVES IN DIFFERENT CLASSIFICATIONS (OF POLITICAL ATTITUDES, EDUCATION, RELIGION) WHO RECOMMEND THAT THE CITY FOLLOW AN INTEGRATED OCCUPANCY PATTERN

	Integrated Interracial Projects				Segregated Bi-Racial Projects			
	Koaltown		Sacktown		Bakerville		Frankville	
Political Attitudes								
Liberal	56%	(34) *	74%	(31)	0%	(18)	12%	(25)
Middle of the road	41	(29)	45	(22)	8	(37)	3	(36)
Conservative	60	(30)	40	(35)	2	(45)	6	(35)
Education								
Only public school	53	(43)	36	(25)	4	(50)	3	(40)
Some high school	54	(28)	40	(30)	3	(33)	6	(33)
Completed high school or had some college .	36	(14)	84	(31)	7	(14)	15	(13)
Religion								
Protestant ...	25	(4)	40	(15)	0	(23)	0	(15)
Catholic	38	(16)	33	(39)	2	(66)	2	(40)
Jewish	58	(72)	78	(23)	29	(7)	10	(38)

* Figures in parentheses indicate the number of cases on which the percentage figures have been computed.

Similar results are obtained if we compare people who are equated simultaneously with respect to education, religion, and political attitudes. For example, let us compare the matched groups we have used in other analyses — the politically conservative Catholics who have had only an elementary school education in the two types of projects. Of the *14* such people in the integrated projects 6 favor integration; none of the 28 such people in Bakerville and Frankville recommend integration. Or if we contrast politically middle-of-the-road Jewish people who have gone to high school, we find comparable results. In the integrated projects 5 out of 8 support integration; in the segregated projects only 1 out of 8 do likewise. The results are similar for whatever equated groups of people are compared. Thus, though the figures are small, the evidence is cumulative. We may conclude that *the housewife's attitudes toward living in interracial housing are markedly influenced by her experiences with interracial housing.*

It is interesting to note that, in all four projects, the Jewish people are relatively the most favorable to a policy of nonsegregation. In contrast to the findings of other chapters, with respect to policy recommendations, in Koaltown the relatively uneducated as well as the more educated Jewish people have essentially similar views. This lack of difference here helps to explain the similarity of the figures for Koaltown and Sacktown in Table 23.

General Reactions to Living in the Projects

While the housewife's attitudes toward interracial relations and her feelings about the project as a place to bring up children may be expected to influence her general opinions about the project, these are not the only factors at work. We must remember that the tenants of these projects, before living in them, were characterized by a dire need for adequate housing. Their admission to the projects, in a sense, is a direct measure of their need, since customarily there are many more applicants than there are available apartments and need is one of the most important criteria used by housing authorities in selecting tenants. Typically they had been living in deteriorated, cold-water flats, with too many people in each room, and under rentals too high for their incomes. The statement of a women in Bakerville summarizes a common reaction in all of the projects to our question, "Why did you move from where you had been living previously?" She replied, "I wanted a better place to live. There was no bath, no hot water, the toilet was outside. It was cold, dark, and not sanitary. There were two families in the same apartment because we couldn't pay the rent."

In housing, as in most aspects of life, one's standard of judgment is very much influenced by what one has been accustomed to and by one's available alternatives. Though from either an esthetic or a family-living point of view the projects we have studied leave much to be desired, they nevertheless are superior to the housing accommodations that are generally in existence for low-income or even many middle-income families. It is, thus, not surprising that the overwhelming majority of the women in all four projects evaluate their projects positively. Yet, as one might expect from our material on racial attitudes, negative evaluations are more common among the women in the segregated than in the integrated projects. In Bakerville, 21 percent and in Frankville 13 percent respond with a strong negative reaction to the project as a whole; in Sacktown the corresponding figure is 10 percent and in Koaltown only 6 percent.

From our interviews, it is apparent that the housewives are particularly pleased with their apartments and with the facilities and service available in the project. They like the fact that their apartments are clean, light, and roomy. There are, of course, objections at many points; e.g., to the composition of the floors (the floors are not made of wood), to the lack of doors on closets, to the dampness of apartments, to the casement windows, or to the lack of freedom to decorate the apartment as they wish. They like the free gas and electricity, the dependable heat and hot water, the maintenance and repairs made by management without constant badgering. Many of them also express a liking for the principle of public housing; except for those who are threatened with eviction because of excessive income, they tend to favor the notion that one's rent should be related to one's income. However, quite a few resent the intrusion on their privacy that comes with living in a publicly supported project — the common knowledge of the level of income checks, the necessity of reporting to management when there is a change in work status, and so on.

The largest source of dissatisfaction, as we have indicated earlier in the chapter, arises from the neighborhoods in which the projects are located. These are almost unanimously disliked. Bad features specifically referred to are the deterioration, the delinquency, the lack of adequate shopping facilities, the schools, and the lack of recreational facilities for the children.

To sum up, in this chapter we have presented material which indicates that the majority of the housewives in the integrated projects respond positively to the interracial aspects of their projects. In contrast, many of the women in Bakerville and Frankville react to the segregated bi-racial occupancy pattern with the perception that they are not living in an interracial project; otherwise their reactions are more likely to be negative than positive. Many of the white housewives in the integrated as well as the segregated projects express doubts about the projects as places to bring up children in; few Negro women have this reaction. The children interviewed in Sacktown, however, seem to be, for the most part, enthusiastic about living in their project. In Bakerville, the children are rather unenthusiastic;

their lack of enthusiasm appears to grow partly out of some indirect consequences of the segregated pattern.

From our data it seems clear that one of the results of living in an integrated occupancy pattern is that one is most likely to favor this pattern when asked to recommend a general policy; living in a segregated bi-racial pattern, however, leads the white housewife to favor even more segregation than that to which she has been exposed in the project. The considerable percentage of housewives who still favor a policy of segregation, even after living in an integrated interracial project, should be a warning against complacency. To be sure, much change will occur, as our results have indicated, in projects with an integrated occupancy pattern. But this alone, particularly when prejudice characterizes the broader community, will not affect all tenants, nor will it cause major changes in all whom it affects in some degree.

CHAPTER XII

Summary and Conclusions

In PRECEDING chapters we have presented evidence which indicates
that there are striking differences with respect to racial relations and
racial attitudes between the residents in two New York integrated
interracial and in two Newark segregated bi-racial housing projects.
The fact of these differences is hardly debatable. However, neither
scientists nor practical men are interested in facts per se; it is the
interpretation and the implications of facts which are of significance.
In this chapter we shall examine further the implications of the facts
we have reported. Before proceeding with this examination a brief review of our major findings may be helpful.

SUMMARY

Two integrated interracial low-rent, public housing projects in New
York City were compared with two similar segregated bi-racial projects in Newark to determine the socio-psychological effects of the
two occupancy patterns upon racial relations and racial attitudes.
The projects in the two cities were selected so as to be matched in
terms of Negro-white ratios and comparable in other relevant respects. Approximately 100 white and 25 Negro housewives were in-
tensively interviewed in each of the four projects. In addition, 24
children between the ages of 11 and 14 years, of both races and of
both sexes, were interviewed in each of the two types of housing
projects.

The integrated interracial projects in comparison with the segregated bi-racial projects were characterized by:

1. Many more instances of friendly, neighborly contacts between
members of the different races.

2. A social atmosphere more favorable to friendly interracial associations.

3. A more closely knit project community.

4. More favorable attitudes toward the Negro people in the project and also toward Negro people in general.

5. More favorable attitudes also toward the Chinese, although here the differences between the two types of projects were smaller.

6. More favorable attitudes toward living in an interracial project.

INTERPRETATION

These behavioral and attitudinal differences between the tenants in the New York and Newark projects seem to result directly from the following differences between the two types of occupancy patterns:

1. The physical and functional proximity of Negro and white families is considerably greater in the integrated than in the segregated projects.

2. The social norms with respect to racial relations implicit in the official policy regarding the type of occupancy pattern by a public authority is more favorable to friendly interracial relations in the integrated than in the segregated bi-racial projects.

3. In a broader social milieu characterized by racial prejudice, the discrepancy between the social norms of the project and those of the broader community is greater for the residents in the integrated projects; it seems likely that this greater discrepancy has drawn the tenants in these projects closer together.

In an *ex post facto* study, such as the present one, change is always inferred rather than directly observed. From the existence of the marked differences in racial attitudes and behavior between the tenants in the integrated interracial projects and those in the segregated bi-racial projects, we *infer* that a considerable number of tenants in the former have become less prejudiced. This inference is supported by the reports of the housewives about their own attitudinal changes: many more women in the integrated than in the segregated projects report favorable attitudinal changes. The findings of related research,[1] which indicate that equal-status contacts with Negroes are likely to reduce prejudices, also lend credibility to our inference. However, without an examination of alternative interpretations of the differences found between the two types of projects, we cannot be reasonably confident of the correctness of our interpretation.

We have reviewed the evidence that we could bring to bear upon

[1] See the previously cited studies by Allport and Kramer, Brophy, Davis, MacKenzie, Rose, and Smith.

the question of the comparability of the interracial experiences and attitudes of the tenants prior to their moving into the two types of projects. All of the evidence — the psychological situation of the low-income family with a dire need for housing, the low rate of refusals by applicants and the low rate of voluntary move-outs by tenants of the various projects we have studied, the reports of the housewives about their attitudes and experiences prior to moving into the projects, and our comparison of housewives in the two types of projects who are similar in education, religion, and political attitudes — all indicate that it is unlikely that the behavioral and attitudinal differences our data have revealed can be "explained away" in terms of an initial lack of comparability of the tenants in the two types of projects. Nor are the differences we found, so far as it is possible to tell, attributable to any idiosyncrasies in the projects we studied: tenant morale is high in all projects, no "special" efforts have been made to produce changes in attitudes in any of the projects, the projects in the two cities are similar in many respects (in ratio of Negroes to whites, in neighborhoods, in eligibility requirements, in age, in possessing interracial staffs, etc.).

Thus, factors other than the occupancy pattern that might explain our results, have been systematically examined and have been found to be inconsistent with the available data. It seems not unreasonable to conclude that *from the point of view of reducing prejudice and of creating harmonious democratic intergroup relations, the net gain resulting from the integrated projects is considerable; from the same point of view, the gain created by the segregated bi-racial projects is slight.*

IMPLICATIONS

In examining the implications of our results we shall ask first about their meaning for interracial housing and then about their significance for intergroup relations in general. In what circumstances should we expect our results to hold for other comparisons of integrated interracial and segregated bi-racial projects? Under what conditions could we recommend the adoption of integrated housing in anticipation of results similar to those we found? From our results what can we conclude about factors affecting intergroup relations outside of public housing?

Implications for interracial housing. As a first step in considering the meaning of our results for interracial housing in general, let us examine the probability that our results would be confirmed in other comparisons of the two types of occupancy pattern. A study by Mer-

ton, West, and Jahoda[2] of (in our terminology) a segregated bi-racial
project in Pittsburgh reports results very similar to the ones we found
for the bi-racial projects we studied in Newark. Our survey of housing officials experienced in interracial housing also supports the impression that the segregated bi-racial project does not afford enough
opportunities for intimate interracial contact to produce major attitudinal changes.

While we have studied integrated projects only in New York, our
interviews with housing officials in different parts of the country certainly suggest that New York is not the only place in which an integrated policy is possible. In such various cities as Hartford, Los
Angeles, Philadelphia, Seattle, and Berkeley, integrated interracial
projects exist and they are managed without difficulties. Though the
population of New York (and of the projects we have studied) is
undoubtedly more polyglot and possibly more tolerant than in other
sections of the country, the residential segregation of Negroes (apart
from public housing) has been more rigid than in many other cities.
Integration thus, in a sense, represents in New York a greater break
with community practices than would be true for many cities. Moreover, the integrated interracial projects we studied in New York are
far from ideal choices to demonstrate the "workability" of integrated
housing. Both projects contain a relatively high proportion of Negro
families, and many housing officials believe that when a project contains a population as high as 40 percent Negro (both of the projects
we studied had at least this proportion) it becomes more difficult for
the white tenants to adjust to living in an integrated project. Both
projects are also located in predominantly Negro neighborhoods,
neighborhoods which are, in addition, rather deteriorated and characterized by considerable delinquency.

Further, although the tenant composition of the New York projects may differ from that to be expected in many other cities, it
should be stressed that no matter what segment of the housewives
we studied is considered, similar results are obtained with respect to
changes in racial relations and racial attitudes. That is, Catholic,
Protestant, and Jew, the politically liberal and politically conservative, and the well educated and poorly educated adjusted to living
in an integrated project and became less prejudiced despite initial
forebodings.

While we see no reason for believing that integration is workable
only in New York, the favorable results we found might not be ex-

[2] See their *Explorations in the Social Psychology of Housing*, being published by
Harper.

pected under the following types of circumstances: where an "integrated" project contains only a token representation of Negroes, or, in other words, if the proportion is too small to result in any considerable amount of interracial contact; where attitudes in the community are extremely hostile, perhaps violently opposed to integrated housing — so much so that it becomes impossible to live in the project without bearing the brunt of the active opposition of the community; where the housing authority and project management do not firmly support and execute a policy of integration without equivocation — where, in other words, "integration" can be subverted by "complaints," by manipulation of management, etc.; where the management staff are prejudiced; or where extremely inefficient management results in low tenant morale, with bickering and hostility characterizing the relationships among tenants of all groups.

In the light of these judgments about the conditions under which our findings might be expected to hold, what can we recommend concerning the use of integrated housing in other cities? Before attempting an answer to this question we should point out that there is the possibility of much confusion in the discussion of the relationship between research and policy decisions. Research can never dictate or be a substitute for basic value judgments; it can only determine, at most, which of several alternatives is likely to lead most effectively to desired objectives. The objectives themselves, except insofar as they are only "means" to further objectives, are beyond the purview of science. In his role as scientist, the social psychologist cannot assert whether, in and of themselves, the reduction of prejudice and the creation of friendly equal-status interracial relations are desirable (though in terms of objectives related to democracy or to international relations, it may be possible for him to make this assertion without violating his scientific role). He can, however, state that if these are desiderata, then under certain conditions, and not others, they will be attained.

Independently of research findings, every individual has the right to search his conscience and make a moral judgment about the desirability of an integrated or a segregated policy. Of course, research results, by extending the factual context and by pointing out consequences, may influence this judgment. However, even if research findings were to indicate that the integrated pattern, under conditions such as exist now in the Deep South, results in "trouble," the ethical principles of many would still lead them to favor the integrated pattern. For these people, the integrated pattern (the elimination of official invidious distinctions between Negroes and whites) may be considered, in itself, an important moral end. Others, guided by our hypothetical research results in the South, may still favor an integrated pattern but will, at the same time, try to create the conditions which will make it result in a reduction of prejudice and in the creation of friendly, equal-status interracial relations. It may well be that striving to create such a policy is one of the most effective means for creating the conditions necessary to its successful execution.

Though we have indicated the possibility that the integrated pattern at this moment of history is not feasible in the Deep South, we must confess to a lack of verified knowledge about this point. Our research has not contributed to an understanding of the socio-political conditions which favor the adoption and the successful execution of an integrated policy. We would, however, hazard the guess that, in most circumstances, if sufficient political power can be obtained by its proponents to result in the adoption of this policy, then sufficient political power exists for its successful execution; the reverse is also probably true — that is, if there is not enough political power for its successful execution, there is not likely to be enough power for its adoption. Possibly the major exception to this statement occurs when the political power resulting in the adoption of a policy has no relevance to its execution (e.g., if the federal government were to ban segregation but the responsibility for its execution were in the hands of local officials in the South) — that is, when there is no firm resolve, backed by enforcement provisions, to execute policy.

We are, in effect, rejecting the notion that has characterized much of sociological thinking in the field of racial relations: the notion, originating with William S. Sumner, that "stateways cannot change folkways." The evidence of our study is that official policy, executed without equivocation, can result in large changes in beliefs and feelings despite initial resistance to the policy. Thus, it is clear from our data that although most of the white housewives in the integrated projects we studied did not, upon moving into the projects, like the idea of living in the same buildings with Negro families (and certainly the community as a whole did not favor it), a considerable change in attitudes and "folkways" has taken place as a consequence of their experiences resulting from a "stateway."

We believe (though additional research is obviously necessary to replace beliefs by verified knowledge) that the socio-political conditions throughout most of the North and in the West are such as to make integrated interracial housing feasible; and in terms of democratic values, if it is feasible, it is preferable, by far, to the segregated bi-racial pattern. The free mixing of Negroes and whites in buses and trolleys, in downtown cinemas and in shopping centers, and, to some extent, in schools and at work, the lack of legal or moral pressures to segregate, and the growing political significance of the Negro vote — all suggest its feasibility in much of the North and West. In contrast, the pervasive "Jim Crow" of the South, the legal and extralegal supports for prejudice and discrimination, the almost complete lack of political rights and of political power by Negroes, and the organized and semilegalized violence to keep Negroes in an inferior status suggest that considerable political-economic change (internally or externally imposed) will be necessary before integration will be either a likely or a feasible policy in much of the South.

Implications for intergroup relations in general. In a sense, we are on considerably firmer ground when we discuss the theoretical implications of our research. Other related studies have been made in rather different social settings in which more or less similar sociopsychological conditions were at work. These studies, which we have previously cited, in the army, in industry, in the merchant marine, in universities, and in government agencies all provide results which are in essential agreement with the results of the present study. They all indicate that under certain types of conditions equal-status contacts with Negroes will result in a considerable change in the behavior and attitudes of the prejudiced person.

What are these conditions? In brief (a more extended, technical discussion is presented in Appendix A) it seems that prejudices are likely to be diminished when prejudiced persons are brought into situations which compel[3] contacts between them and the objects of prejudice, provided that:

1. The behavior of the objects of prejudice is such as to be at variance or not to conform, with the beliefs of the prejudiced. That is, the Negroes, with whom the prejudiced person has contact, are not "lazy," "ignorant," "delinquent," etc.

2. The intimacy and amount of contact with the objects of prejudice, not conforming to the stereotypes of the prejudiced, are such as to result in experiences which are sufficiently compelling to resist marked perceptual and memorial distortion.

3. The contact takes place under conditions which make the nonconforming behavior seem relevant to the basis on which the objects of prejudice are grouped together. Thus, even though a Negro attendant is seen to be clean and honest, there may be little effect on stereo-

---

[3] "Compel" either because of ecological factors, such as in an interracial housing project, or because of compelling individual goals, such as a desire to use a swimming pool open to all groups.

types if the perception of cleanliness and honesty is connected primarily with the requirements of the situation, with the classification of the individual as an attendant rather than as a Negro or Negro attendant.[4]

4. The prejudiced person has values or is exposed to social influences (e.g., democratic values or the social influences emanating from a policy of an official, public body) which would strongly conflict with the unabashed retention of unrationalized prejudices.

In addition, if the contact situation is such that it encourages the development of new sentiments to replace prejudiced sentiments either as a result of the experience of cooperative activity with the objects of prejudice or as a result of the internalization of the social norms of an unprejudiced group, the reduction of prejudiced sentiments will be much facilitated.

[4] Just as there is likely to be little effect upon prejudiced beliefs if "good" behavior upon the part of the objects of prejudice is seen to result from the requirements of the situation rather than from the person or from the person's membership in a minority group, so, too, one can expect a reduction in prejudice if "bad" behavior upon their part comes to be seen as emanating from their circumstances rather than from their personality or minority group membership. This is why changes in theories of behavior (from a genetic to an environmental emphasis) may have a subtle influence even upon prejudice.

Postscript

A NEW policy for locating tenants is now in effect in Newark's eight public housing projects and will also apply to the three skyscraper developments soon to be constructed. That policy, one long favored by many of us, provides that henceforth all apartments are to be allocated on a basis of need, regardless of race, religion, and color. As a result, the partial segregation which has characterized public housing in Newark will no longer obtain. Instead of Negroes and whites being kept in separate buildings, they are being assigned to apartments in the same buildings without regard to their race.

In large measure, this change in fundamental policy reflects the impact of the study reported in this book. The study has served as a catalyst to the re-examination of our basic interracial policies in housing and as a stimulus to their change. Many of us have long felt that the artificial separation of Negro and white families was an unwholesome procedure. However, until the study of Dr. Deutsch and Mrs. Collins, we had no scientific evidence to substantiate our feelings. In supplying us with an objective picture of race relations in our projects, a picture which is faithful to our own impressions, their study dramatically focused our attention and that of the community at large on matters which, under the press of other business, we had tended to ignore.

The study did more than help to focus attention on the basic question of segregation in housing. Perhaps its most important consequence was its usefulness to those community groups concerned with intergroup relations and civil rights, such as the Essex County Intergroup Council. To such groups the study was an invaluable tool in creating the atmosphere which made it possible for the housing authority to adopt and execute a policy of nonsegregation. I don't know how many meetings of such groups I attended, but invariably the

Deutsch-Collins study was referred to and quoted. All these meetings were necessary and helpful. Without active support from community groups and the new state law prohibiting discrimination in public housing, it would have been extremely difficult for us to adopt a change in policy.

A word about the change. Naturally, as we undertook the process of integrating our projects, we were beset by some anxieties. If, however, our Newark experience may serve as a guide, the change-over to a policy of nonsegregation is not so difficult and troublesome as one anticipates. Some of our tenants (these are by far in the minority) have complained to us vociferously, but there has been no disruption of our projects. When the complainants met a firm, calm response from housing management, they invariably subsided. Our experience leads me to believe that if a housing authority, its executive director and his staff, show complete sincerity in the change and never retreat from their announced position with respect to nonsegregation, the change will be successful. This, in any case, is what we have found to be true in Newark.

Even in this short time we have already observed significant changes in attitudes, as a consequence of which we shall undoubtedly find that as we break down the physical barriers between Negroes and whites in our projects, many of the social barriers will also disappear. We have been pleasantly surprised to find that some of the white tenants who were loudest in their objections to living next to Negro families have come to accept as *neighbors* the Negro families living next to them.

Louis Danzig
Executive Director, Housing Authority of
the City of Newark

November 1950

The Nature of Prejudice

THE socio-psychological nature of prejudice, the methods by which it is perpetuated, and the conditions necessary to its change have been subjects of considerable study by social scientists. Any single piece of research, such as the present one, must necessarily be relevant to only a small segment of the thinking that has been done in this area. Yet in the course of working through this study, developing hypotheses, constructing questionnaires, and analyzing our results, we found it advantageous to keep before us the major assumptions underlying theoretical work being done in this area.[1] Perhaps the reader will find it profitable if we present, in brief, these assumptions as we view them.

There are two vantage points from which prejudice may be viewed. One point of view focuses upon the functions that it fulfills for the individual — this is the psychological approach; the other stresses the social origins and social functions of prejudice — this is the sociological approach. Though in the writings of many theorists there has been a tendency to emphasize one approach to the neglect of the other, there is no necessary opposition between these two focuses; basically, they are complementary. Indeed, all social groups or societies, no matter how large or small, require for their effective functioning that the individuals composing them develop attitudes which predispose them to behave in accordance with their respective roles in the fulfillment of group purposes.

There is considerable evidence that prejudice has the social "func-

[1] No attempt will be made to credit all the various authors that have helped to clarify thinking in this field. Writings by Allport and Kramer (1), Cox (4), Festinger (7), Krech and Crutchfield (10), Lewin (11), Murphy (17), Murray and Morgan (18), Newcomb (20), Smith (22), and Tolman (24) have been particularly helpful. (Throughout Appendix A the numbers within parentheses refer to the bibliography at the end of it.)

tion"[2] of buttressing the social practices of exploitation, political discrimination, and segregation. The attribution of innate inferiority to a group that is physically distinguishable is a relatively modern phenomenon deriving from a need to have a rationale for exploitative practices and for invidious distinctions in an era in which the moral doctrine of "liberty, equality, and fraternity" was being proudly proclaimed.

Thus, Myrdal has written (19, p. 89): "The fateful word *race* itself is actually not yet two hundred years old. The biological ideology had to be utilized as an intellectual explanation of, and moral apology for, slavery in a society which went out emphatically to invoke as its highest principles the ideals of the inalienable rights of all men to freedom and equality of opportunity. It was born out of the conflict between an old harshly non-equalitarian institution — which was not, or perhaps in a short time could not be, erased — and the new shining faith in human liberty and democracy. The race dogma is nearly the only way out for a people if it is not prepared to live up to its faith. A nation less fervently committed to democracy could, probably, live happily in a caste system with a somewhat less intensive belief in the biological inferiority of the subordinate group. The need for race prejudice is, from this point of view, a need for defense on the part of Americans against their own national creed, against their own most cherished ideals."

However, racial prejudice not only serves as a means of justifying the exploitative practices of socially influential groups in the face of conflicting democratic values; it also functions to perpetuate the conditions necessary for continued exploitation. It provides attitudinal support for the social practices of segregation and of discrimination which serve to prevent Negroes from achieving equality and from rising in status and which hinder the development of feelings of solidarity or common purposes between Negroes and whites.

Perhaps the nature of prejudice will be clarified by its comparison with "intolerance." Intolerance differs from prejudice in that its primary social function is conversion or extirpation rather than exploitation. The dominant group is intolerant of those whom it can define as antisocial, divisive, or socially disrupting — e.g., the criminal, the religious minority, the nonconformist, and the political extremist;

[2] We are using the word "function," throughout the Appendix, in a somewhat different sense from that used popularly (16). We do not mean to imply any conscious intent or deliberate plan, though there is no doubt that prejudice is deliberately fostered by some groups to facilitate the achievement of their ends. Rather, we mean it to denote that an activity or social institution or social attitude has an immanent social consequence (which may or may not be "deliberate" or "conscious").

it is prejudiced against those whom it can define as being unworthy
of or incapable of being equal. (This is not to deny that intolerance
may under certain social conditions "evolve" into prejudice.) To put
it in other words, the condition of the dominant group's liking the
nonconformist is that he cease being a nonconformist and voluntarily
become like the generality of society, while the condition of its liking
the Negro is that he cease trying to become like the rest of society
and remain contentedly in an inferior position (4).

While it is clear that racial prejudice originated as a means of
justifying and maintaining an economic function for socially influential groups and that the social institution of slavery was effectively
challenged only when it became dysfunctional to more powerful economic interests, for many it has not been clear that prejudice still
functions economically to exploit Negro labor. This is not to say that
all segments of society share equally in the fruits of this exploitation
or that, from an over-all perspective of the total American economy,
this exploitation is economical. Yet, powerful political and economic
groups in the North as well as in the South directly benefit from the
rewards of exploitation and indirectly from prejudices which prevent
the development of feelings of solidarity between Negro and white
workers. For the less powerful and more populous groups which no
longer have (or never had) an economic or political stake in prejudice, prejudices serve the less "rational" functions of preserving or
enhancing ego and social status.

Although there is accumulating evidence to indicate that social institutions and the attitudes buttressing them are likely to change
when they no longer serve their prime purpose (and that the social
change — which our study also gives evidence of — is usually prior
to the attitudinal change), it is not uncommon to find that social
institutions and their complementary attitudes become independent
of their originating functions. Partly this is true today with respect
to the practices of segregation and discrimination and with respect to
prejudice. They have gathered a momentum of their own which has
made them independent of their initial political and economic functions.

It is of considerable social importance to understand how these
practices and attitudes tend to perpetuate themselves and what are
the means of undoing what has been so aptly named the "vicious
circle." To this purpose, we wish to present a more detailed discussion
of the nature of prejudice as a social attitude and of the conditions
which tend toward its perpetuation independently of its initial functions.

I

Prejudice, like most attitudes, can be considered as consisting of several major interrelated components (23):

1. First of all, an attitude is relevant to some aspect of the individual's environment (such as a person, a group, an idea, an ideology, a place, an institution, or an activity). It may refer to a narrow or broad range of entities in the environment — to only dark-skinned Negroes or to all people who have a Negro ancestor. The identification of the content or scope of an attitude largely takes place through study of the goals of behavior. To the extent that one entity is substitutable for another as a goal-object, they tend to be subsumed under the same attitude.

A distinctive characteristic of group, in contrast to individual, prejudices is that the objects of prejudice are socially, rather than individually, defined. Thus, all people labeled "Negro" or "Jewish" may be lumped into their respective categories no matter how varied and individually distinctive these people may be otherwise. Under certain conditions, a rough measure of the strength of a group prejudice is the extent to which "categories" related to prejudice are more influential than other bases of classifying people. It should be emphasized that it is the existing social definitions of "Negro" or "Jewish," rather than any scientific analysis of racial or cultural similarities, which is the determining factor in the categorization. The inclusiveness of the social definition is a function, in part, of the requirements of the exploitative situation and, in part, of the kinds of objective clues which exist for the identification of any group that is socially defined as an object of prejudice. A rigid adherence to the social definition is a social "necessity" (deviations from this adherence are likely to incur group sanctions) to prevent the possible breakdown of the exploitative situation via either assimilation or the development of feelings of solidarity with individual members of a minority group which might then be generalized to the group as a whole. Our results certainly indicate that such generalization may take place to Negroes-in-general from intimate contacts with only a limited number of Negro people.[3]

[3] There are, of course, prejudiced individuals who are friendly with people who fit into the social definition of "Negro." Typically such people exclude their Negro friends from the Negro group: "They are an exception" or "I don't think of them as Negroes." In effect, they deny the group identification of their friends. In contrast, an unprejudiced person instead of denying his friend's group identification denies the social distinction between Negroes and whites, with some such statement as "It makes no difference to me whether a person is Negro or white." Or, perhaps, he affirms his liking for his *Negro* friend (with whatever cultural and physical uniqueness he has as a Negro) just as he might express a liking for a specific *French* film.

2. Second, an attitude is motivationally relevant. It consists of sentiments which predispose the individual to perceive or anticipate certain motivationally relevant relationships between himself and a specified entity and thus to react affectively to the given entity. The quality and direction of the affect (love, sympathy, pity, hate, fear, etc.) displayed in any particular situation will depend upon the type of motivation that is acting upon the individual and upon the motivational relationships (frustrating or gratifying) anticipated in the situation; the strength of the affect will depend upon the strength of the motivation, the strength of the sentiment, and certain field relationships (potency, relative position, etc.).

The distinctive characteristics of prejudiced sentiments arise, as one might expect, from the social practices they serve to buttress. In part, the sentiments will vary in accordance with the general context of racial relations — e.g., whether the Negro is in the majority of the population (as in South Africa) or not — but the basic core of such sentiments is inextricably connected with the motivational nexus related to social status. The prejudiced person anticipates that any significant rise in the social status of Negroes (i.e., in eligibility to receive the rewards deemed valuable in a given society) is likely to be negatively interrelated with the likelihood of his obtaining or maintaining what he considers to be a satisfactory social status for himself. This is why the prejudiced person is predisposed to respond with hostility or aggression (or when they expect to be successfully challenged by the Negro, with "fear") to Negroes if they seek either equal status or a relative advancement in status; in contrast, if the Negro is content to remain subservient, if he is happy though exploited, if he is deferent or self-abasing, and thus relatively enhances the status of the white, the prejudiced person will react with positive or benign affect. Theories of prejudice have too frequently stressed hostility as the underlying sentiment; hostility is, however, only one of the many affective reactions which may be evoked by what we have termed "the prejudiced sentiment." The particular affective reaction to be expected from a prejudiced person is a function not only of his sentiments but of the particular motivational relationship between him and his object of prejudice in a specific situation at a given time.

3. In addition to the motivationally relevant expectations regarding an entity, an attitude usually involves other expectations or beliefs about the entity. These beliefs may help to assign an entity to a specific motivationally relevant category (thus, the belief that antihistamine tablets prevent colds may make these tablets a goal-object

under certain motivational conditions) and be the basis for the development of sentiments or they may provide a rationale for the already existing (e.g., culturally determined) motivational relevance of an entity.

In the latter instance the beliefs or rationales serve to justify the existing sentiments in the face of challenge from the environment or to insulate them from other sentiments or values with which they might be in conflict. They do this by establishing an apparent relationship of dependence between the challenged sentiments and the more basic sentiments or values that are accepted by the culture or the individual without question; by so doing, the challenged sentiments receive the support of these more basic structures. It is, of course, possible for sentiments to exist without rationales if the environment or internalized value provides no resistance. Thus, we may benignly regard the mule as a beast of burden without elaborate rationalization or without qualm since we incur no internal or external opposition to using the mule in this manner.

However, in a democratic society which holds "equality" as one of its main values, it is likely that the challenges to prejudiced sentiments will require that they be supported by fairly elaborate rationales. We have previously indicated the function of the belief in the innate or biological inferiority of Negroes in justifying the social institution of slavery and the harshly nonequalitarian practices of the ante-bellum South. A thorough examination of the beliefs which support prejudice would undoubtedly show that they are as varied as the situations which require defense in the face of moral challenge. Practically every type of Negro-white relation, every type of discriminatory practice, every type of interracial policy, raises its own unique demands for justification and results in the development of its own special set of rationalizing beliefs. Thus, "The beliefs that Negroes get sleepy when working with machines and that they, on the whole, lack mechanical aptitudes, serve a need for justification of their being kept out of industry. . . . The beliefs that the Negro race is 'childish,' immature, undeveloped, servile, lacking in initiative, are used to justify the denial of full civil rights and suffrage to Negroes. . . . The beliefs that Negroes have a much smaller cranial capacity and lower brain weight, a less complicated brain structure, thicker skull bones . . . have a function to explain and fortify the beliefs in . . . his lower intelligence and reasoning power." (19, pp. 106–7)

Beliefs pile upon beliefs, so that many prejudiced individuals have an imposing structure of rationales to support their sentiments. Despite their frequently impressive elaborateness, there is much evidence

to indicate that, for most people, beliefs are more superficial than underlying sentiments. Their opportunistic nature, the logical inconsistency of many of the beliefs held by any one prejudiced individual, the
way they shift under external pressure, research results (such as ours)
which suggest that beliefs change more readily than feelings — all
of these intimate that for most prejudiced people beliefs are rational-
istic rather than rational.

4. In relation to any entity toward which he is affectively predisposed, the individual tends to develop an action orientation which
consists of a pattern of action policies that serve to guide the individual's actions in specific situations. These policies are developed to
accord with what the individual comes to believe as being feasible in
the existing reality, on the one hand, and with his sentiments and
rationales on the other. Thus, an unprejudiced person in face of the
existing social pressures against being friendly with Negroes may act
in a manner resembling that of a prejudiced person. For example, to
avoid unpleasant social repercussions he may avoid entertaining Negro friends at his home, or, in the South, he may conform to "Jim
Crow" practices. Since interracial relations is such a salient social
issue in the United States, strong social pressures are exerted to make
individuals conform to the accepted social norms for interracial behavior. This is the reason why the conformity needs of the individual
typically play such an important role in determining his action orientation with respect to race relations.

While it is beyond the purposes of this appendix to elaborate other
characteristics of the attitude of prejudice, certain basic points should
be noted: (a) An attitude is a dynamic organization in which the
component parts are continuously interacting. (b) As an attitude,
prejudice is not necessarily an isolated dynamic system; it may be
subordinate to or dominant over other related dynamic systems. It
is primarily because prejudice is not an isolated system that personality factors may markedly influence the individual's susceptibility to
its influences; frequently, it flourishes upon a soil of repressed hostili-
ties or insecurities with respect to status. (c) As a more or less enduring organization, an attitude tends to maintain an organizational
stability by influencing perceptual, memorial, and effector processes
so as to reject, isolate, distort, or ignore disrupting experiences.

II

In an earlier section of this appendix, we indicated that the social
practices of discrimination and segregation and the attitude of prejudice which support these practices originally had (and to a large

extent still have) the "function" of placing the objects of prejudice at a disadvantage both in the attainment of goals which are desired by the prejudiced and in the acquisition of the means, skills, values, etc. necessary to the attainment of such goals.

Members of a minority group may, as a consequence of being placed in a disadvantageous position, develop certain social and psychological characteristics which, in turn, may function to support the rationales for prejudiced sentiments. It is instructive to consider historically the barriers posed to prevent Negroes from participating freely in the culture of the white man and to examine their sociopsychological effects upon the Negro group. The Negro slave "could not vote, serve on juries, take part in legislatures or hold office. He could not own land and a home and establish a business. He could not go out as a pioneer, hunter, trapper, surveyor, mining prospector. He could not offer his labor in a free competitive market. He could not make a marriage recognized by law or have the right to keep with him his wife and children. He could not assume responsibility for the support of his family and authority over his children. They were the property of his wife's master to do with as he pleased. He could not defend the sanctity of his women. Their purity and chastity was not something to be honored. On the contrary, easy animal compliance in the Negro slave woman was an object and an advantage to the master class and was to be rewarded; personal chastity was an annoyance and to be broken down. Enterprise, initiative, independence, an alert belligerent sense of personal freedom and personal honor — which were set great store by in the white community — were the exact opposite of the values commended and rewarded in the slave. In him it was virtue to be obedient to command, to be docile and unquestioning, to show child-like trust, compliance, smoothness, servility, happy acceptance of any fate." (15, p. 17)

In large measure these conditions, which existed under slavery, still exist today. The average Negro denied opportunity for advancement in employment, "the last to be hired and the first to be fired," has to have remarkable persistence to maintain ambition; discriminated against in education, without the economic means to avail himself of it when it exists, without the prospects of vocational or other reward for his studiousness, he has to have unusual perseverance to become well educated; living in restricted slums, under oppressive conditions, forced to menial work away from her home and her children, the Negro housewife must have striking ingenuity and fortitude to be able to keep a clean, well-kept home and to prevent her children from falling into evil ways.

Thus, the social practices of discrimination and segregation help to determine this environment in which Negroes must live; the environment shapes the culture of the Negroes, determines their values, and influences their behavior. Since this environment is different from that which the average white person experiences, he is estranged by the Negro culture and Negro behavior. Further, guided largely by outmoded biological theories which overemphasize the influence of heredity upon behavior, he interprets the differences between Negroes and whites as reflecting innate differences and ignores the causal significance of his actions in determining the environment to which Negroes make their adjustment. Unfortunately, not only do whites receive support for their rationales by the conditions which they create, but also some Negroes come to accept as valid the rationales of the whites: A Negro convinced of his own inferiority, or of the inferiority of the people with whom he is identified, is not likely to be a militant advocate of Negro rights, nor is he likely to promote the solidarity of the Negro group.

III

The social policies by which Negroes are placed at a disadvantage (discrimination, segregation, exclusion, etc.) and the attitudes of the prejudiced reduce generally the amount of contact between Negroes and whites and place such selective contacts as do take place in an institutionalized frame of reference which tends to fix the perception of relationships in advance in such a way that Negroes are perceived to be of inferior status. Typically, Negroes are limited to close contacts with whites only in such low-status roles as those of menials and servants. But even if a Negro, after overcoming many discriminatory obstacles, manages to become, for example, a skilled surgeon, it is unlikely that many white people will see him functioning in his high-status role. His practice will be confined to Negro hospitals and his professional contacts with white doctors will be considerably limited. Further, it is obvious that a prejudiced person would selectively avoid any contacts which imply that Negroes have equal or higher status. He would not go to a Negro doctor or, if by circumstance he did, he would reverse the usual doctor-patient relationship and treat the doctor as a menial. Generally his relationships with Negroes would be limited to those which would not disrupt his stereotypes. (8)

IV

The consequences of the reduction in amount of contact, of the institutionalization of unequal status contacts, and of the socio-economic plight of the Negro group are such as to provide the experiences which will, in large measure, support the rationales for prejudiced sentiments. Support comes not only from contacts with Negroes of depressed status, but also from contact with the social practices of segregation and discrimination and from contacts with the "experiences," sentiments, and rationales of other prejudiced members of one's own group.

1. The social practices of segregation (as well as those of discrimination) provide powerful reinforcements and stimulations to prejudices. From a socio-psychological point of view the "separate but equal" doctrine is extremely naive. Separation, in itself, implies that the distinguishing of "Negroes" and "whites" is morally and legally an appropriate procedure. It implies a distinction between the groups separated and provides a social basis for classifying individuals; in a sense, it increases the "visibility" of individuals for purposes of social identification. Thus, the Nuremburg laws of Nazi Germany increased the visual distinctiveness between "Aryans" and Jews by forcing Jews to wear differentiating identification. In a very similar way, the visibility of "Negroes" as "Negroes" is very much enhanced by "Jim Crow" laws and practices which keep Negroes and whites from mixing freely. In countries where people of different races and color freely intermingle, the visual distinctiveness of color as a mark of social identification is very much reduced. On the face of it, our assertion that the "seeing" of skin color is largely a function of existing social distinctions rather than something which, in itself, is perceptually natural, may be surprising.[4] However, consider only how visually prominent red hair would be, if "redheads" were forced to sit in the rear sections of buses, were confined to certain residential areas, or were limited to low-status occupations.

Not only does segregation facilitate the distinguishing of Negroes and whites (and also psychologically, the grouping of individual "Negroes" in terms of the existing social definition of the group) but it does more. It helps to perpetuate an invidious distinction between Negroes and whites. In the context of the history of race relations, the distinction connotes Negro inferiority, and, as our results have indicated, it further implies that intimate, equal-status, social relations between members of the two groups are undesirable. In practice, segregation does more than imply, it asserts: both legal and nonlegal

[4] An experiment by Lindzey and Rogolsky has indicated similar results for the visual identification of Jews. People for whom the social identification of Jews is important (i.e., anti-Semites) are more alert to the perception of Jews than are people for whom the social identification is unimportant. (13)

pressures are exerted to keep Negroes and whites apart. Further, in operation, segregation always reflects the inferior status of Negroes. The decision to segregate is made by whites without the consultation or approval of Negroes. The rules which guide segregated behavior are countless; they vary from circumstance to circumstance, but they all conform to one basic purpose — to maintain the "superiority" of the white and the "inferiority" of the Negro. Thus, in accordance with the rules in the South, a white person may walk into a Negro's house by the front door, but a Negro must enter a white person's house by the rear; a white person may call a Negro by his first name, but a Negro dare not do the same to the white person; a white person may hire a Negro to do menial or domestic work, but a Negro person, even if he were financially able, could not similarly employ a white person.

The very existence of these social practices strongly buttresses the rationales for prejudice since behavior tends to be rationalized; one does not like to believe that one's behavior is "irrational" or "immoral." If social custom leads one to avoid intimate contact with Negroes, then Negroes are obviously not the kind of people one would like to be intimate with. If Negroes are customarily treated as inferiors, then it is because they are people who are inferior and who should be treated as inferiors. These rationalizations of behavior receive support from the fact that segregation with all its invidious connotations receives official public sanction. Not only do the "best" people avoid social relations with Negroes but the government, the official public, sanctions segregation in law and in public policy. We have seen in our study how the policy decisions of a housing authority may affect the social norms for race relations in the housing project. There is little doubt that public laws and official policies do provide a standard of behavior; by providing a standard favorable to nonsegregated interracial relations they help to stimulate such behavior. There is evidence in our data that once a change in behavior has occurred, a change in beliefs is likely to follow.

2. Earlier, we have indicated that one of the consequences of segregation is that it generally reduces the amount of contact between Negroes and whites. As a result, for many white people, the main source of information about Negroes comes through contact with the attitudes held by the bigoted. In Chapter V we have pointed out how prejudice may be acquired through contagion from newspapers, comic books, movies, teachers, pulp magazines, etc. Not only do prejudiced attitudes spread bias, but they also serve to reinforce it. The narrowminded individual who reads a sensationally written story about a

crime committed by a Negro or hears his friend tell a joke about "Sambo" receives confirmation of his beliefs. In effect, members of a group that share prejudices in common, through contact with each other, mutually tend to confirm and reinforce each other's beliefs. Since, under the influence of their biases, prejudiced individuals selectively avoid the kinds of experiences which are likely to disrupt their attitudes, a more or less closed social system, or, as Murphy has termed it, a "socially shared autism" develops which tends to be self-perpetuating.

v

Intra-group contact also facilitates the formation of social norms and thus even further helps to promote uniformity of attitudes within a social group. Deviation from these norms beyond certain limits is difficult for the individual because deviation may incur group sanctions. Since deviation in overt behavior is most likely to incur group sanctions, it is possible for an individual to have a "prejudiced" action orientation without having sentiments or rationales appropriate to this orientation. Thus, under certain conditions, it is possible for a group to be considerably more prejudiced in action than in sentiment. This is likely to happen when each member of the group, expecting hostility from other members for "deviating behavior," fails to express or communciate his views and yet allows his actions to be guided by what he thinks the group would approve. The consequence is that, behaviorally, the members are considerably more prejudiced than they would be if they all were able to communicate freely their sentiments to one another.

The "big lie," the sensational accusation, the emotional charge, the violent attack of the professional hatemongers are, in part, based upon an awareness of this social dynamic. Their purpose is to create a social atmosphere in which the individual comes to believe that it is socially dangerous to deviate from the standard of behavior that the hatemongers are trying to create. Since most unprejudiced people are relatively passive in the defense of their beliefs in comparison to the bigots with their militancy (hate, by its very nature, seems to lead to more violent and vigorous activity than do the more benign affects — though this is not the only factor at work), it is probably not uncommon for a militant prejudiced minority to determine the social practices of the unprejudiced majority.

To sum up our argument to this point, we have indicated how racial prejudice originated as a means of justifying and buttressing social practices which had, for socially influential groups, the economic function of the exploitation of Negro labor. Elaborate rationales were necessary to justify these practices in the face of the democratic principles which were being widely proclaimed by the rising mercantile and industrial interests in their struggle to overthrow the feudal nobility. With time some of the original economic value of the exploitation of Negro labor has diminished; yet prejudice and the social practices on which it is based still flourish despite the loss of much of their initial function. We have analyzed in some detail the way the various social practices of discrimination, exclusion, and segregation tend to create the conditions for the continuation of prejudices and how prejudices function so as to perpetuate these social practices. In effect, a vicious circle has been established in which social practices and social attitudes mutually support and reinforce each other so that they perpetuate themselves independently of the loss of some of their originating purpose.[5]

What can be done to break or reverse this vicious circle? Where should efforts be concentrated? What is a rational strategy for solution of the problems of prejudice and discrimination? These are vital questions, the answers to which would involve ethical, economic, and political knowledge which are beyond our competence. Nevertheless, certain suggestions can be made from a socio-psychological point of view.

Our analysis of prejudice and discrimination suggests that any strategy of modifying race relations must have, at least, a fivefold objective: (a) a change in the political-economic relations in our society so that discrimination and prejudice come to fulfill no important purpose for socially influential groups, or, in other words, an elimination of the political-economic motivation and instigation to discrimination and prejudice; (b) a change in the objective socio-economic status of Negroes so that they may have full opportunity to participate in and contribute to the over-all American culture, so that they do not as a group bear the stigmata of discrimination and deprivation; (c) an elimination of the social practices of discrimination, exclusion, and segregation which serve to put Negroes at a social disadvantage and which act as a powerful reinforcement to prejudice; (d) destruction of prejudiced attitudes which predispose the individual to discriminatory behavior and to the support of segregation;

[5] It is doubtful that these social practices and social attitudes could continue themselves indefinitely without some political-economic function for socially influential groups; the conflicting values of democracy would probably over a period of time (if the driving force were lost) act as a brake to slow down and stop the perpetuation of these particular practices and attitudes.

and (e) the development of stronger allegiance to the democratic ideology.

These objectives are all highly interrelated, and there is little doubt that an advance in relation to one is likely to bring along with it an advance in relation to the others (19). An ideal situation would call for abundant efforts on all "fronts" to achieve the desired results. Strategy, however, is called into play because abundant efforts are not available and resources must be used economically if the available effort is to have its maximum result. Strategy is, in essence, a theory of operations which guides behavior in specific situations. The specific behavior, or tactics, may vary widely from situation to situation, and it is a mistake to assume that tactics which are appropriate to one situation (e.g., in the South) will be appropriate to another (e.g., in the North). The successful application of tactics requires both a sound theory of operations and a sound diagnosis of the requirements of the specific situation.

Unfortunately, no developed theory of operations exists, and we are not able to offer one. However, our research and the theoretical analysis of the supports for prejudice offer suggestions about the conditions necessary for a change in attitudes which may have some relevance to such a theory.

Perhaps the first problem which arises in changing prejudiced attitudes is that of bringing to bear upon the prejudiced the experiences necessary to a change in attitudes: "Every opportunity must be seized to utilize the diverse factors which cause inconsistency in attitudes and behavior, if the prejudiced person's attitudes are to be changed. This means that the individual's needs, conformity pressures, etc. must be utilized to bring the prejudiced person into situations which he would selectively avoid if he were guided solely by his prejudiced attitude." [6] For example, a prejudiced person's need for a college degree may expose him to information which is counter to his beliefs, his need for housing may make him move into an interracial housing project during a housing shortage, the operation of a Fair Employment Practices Law may "compel" him to work with Negroes as fellow employees, etc.

Thus, in a sense, the first step in any program to change attitudes must inevitably be directed toward a change in social practices — a change which will create the situations to which a prejudiced person must expose himself if he wishes to satisfy certain of his needs. A change in social practices will, of course, not only create such situa-

[6] I. Chein, "The Problems of Inconsistency," *Journal of Social Issues*, 5, No. 3:52–61.

tions, but it will also help to reduce prejudice by improving the objective socio-economic status of Negroes and by decreasing the social supports of prejudice. Let us analyze the psychological requirements for a situation if it is to result in a reduction of prejudice.

For a disruption in *rationales of prejudice* to occur, the biased individual must be exposed to experiences (a) which contradict the rationales, (b) which are of sufficient intimacy and duration so as to be compelling enough to resist marked perceptual and memorial distortion, and (c) which seem relevant to the basis on which the objects of prejudice are grouped together. In theory, there are an infinite number of ways in which these requirements can be met — a course in race relations, attending a concert by Marian Anderson, a film, etc. — but in reality few situations are both *intense* enough and *generalized* enough to result in large-scale change in the beliefs which support prejudice. The results of our study and of others (2, 9, 14, 22) indicate that one of the most effective experiences in disrupting the rationales of prejudice arises through intimate, equal-status contact with Negroes (who, of course, do not conform to the stereotypes). This latter type of experience is particularly effective both because of its "perceptual" intensity and because of the strength of the motivation to accept as real one's perceptions and experiences. If they are not customarily accepted, the individual would be in a state of continuous insecurity and indecision.

When the "reality of one's own senses and experiences" challenges the rationales for prejudiced sentiments, in effect a conflict situation arises for the individual since the prejudiced sentiments are no longer insulated from other conflicting values or from the conflicting environment. The disruption of rationales thus creates an opportunity for a change in sentiments.

However, there are many ways in which the conflict induced as a consequence of the disruption of rationales may be resolved: (a) Where the prejudiced sentiments are strong, new supplementary rationales may be developed to reinforce the prejudiced feelings. (b) The rationale-disrupting experiences may be isolated, e.g., by whites who say, "The Negro families who live in this project are nice but they are specially selected." (c) The individual may eliminate conflict by withdrawing from contact, thus preventing himself from having further disrupting experiences. (d) The individual may seek additional social support selectively to reinforce his sentiments — "They aren't my friends unless they have the same feelings toward Negroes as I do." (e) The prejudiced feelings may be diminished and replaced by more positive sentiments.

The resolution of the conflict is likely to depend upon many factors, among which are these:

1. The nature of the relation for the individual of the prejudiced sentiments and rationales — i.e., whether the prejudiced sentiments depend upon the classification of an individual as "inferior" or whether the sentiments determine the negative classification. Thus, if the sentiments are the instigators of the rationales, one would expect the prejudiced person to display versatility in developing new rationales as his old ones are shattered; on the other hand, if the rationales are primary (one could expect this, on theoretical grounds, to be relatively infrequent) the prejudiced sentiments should change readily when their rationales are disrupted.

2. The personality of the individual and his modes of adjustment to conflict. By this we mean to imply, simply, that the individual in the course of his life history tends to develop characteristic ways of handling conflict — for example, by regression, escape from the field, compromise, externalization, indecision, or projection. His modes of adjustment to conflict, which are usually considered in relation to clinical problems, are clearly relevant to problems of attitudinal change.

3. The relative strength of the factors in conflict. Here many different kinds of factors are involved directly or indirectly:

a. The strength of the needs and value systems which help to support or conflict with the prejudiced sentiments as a function of both more enduring personality characteristics and temporary situational factors. Thus, an individual who is strongly predisposed to prejudice by deeply rooted insecurities and frustrations is not so likely as others to resolve his conflict in an unprejudiced direction.

b. The social influences of friends, family, authorities, etc. in determining the sentiments and values of the individual. It is hard to overestimate the importance of social influences in determining the individual's behavior. "Only by anchoring his own conduct in something as large, substantial, and superindividual as the culture of the group can the individual stabilize his new beliefs sufficiently to keep them immune from day-by-day fluctuations of moods and influences to which he, as an individual, is subject." (12) This is why attempts to change significant social attitudes must be directed not only toward the individual, but also toward the social institutions and social norms which determine the individual's values and which help to induce the goals for which he strives. Isolated individuals may perhaps change their attitudes as a function of their individual experiences, but the person who is deeply enmeshed in the social life of his com-

munity is unlikely to be able to resist the pressures to conform on
matters of community importance if he wishes to continue in good
social standing. The marked influence of the social milieu is attested
to by the rapidity with which the child sheds his prejudices in a new
environment — e.g., in an interracial camp, in which the social norms
are anti-prejudice — and by the quickness with which he regains them
if he goes back to a prejudiced environment without social support
for his newly formed attitudes.

Any attempt to change the vital social attitudes of an individual
should also, at the same time, try to give him social supports which
will reinforce him in his change. Thus, in part, the effectiveness of
the integrated interracial project in reducing prejudices comes not
only from the favorable social norms induced by the official policy
decision, but also from the fact that the people who change reinforce
each other in their new attitudes; in effect, not only is there an individual change, but there is also a group or cultural change. The
individual, by changing, does not isolate himself; on the contrary, by
not changing he is likely to find himself at odds with his fellow residents. Of course, the project community is itself not completely de-
tached from the broader community and the social influences emanating from it. There is little doubt that one of the factors limiting
the reduction in prejudice among the tenants was these latter influences which were generally counter to the influences of the project.
Under certain circumstances, such as perhaps exist now in much of the
South, the social pressures originating in the broader community
may be so strongly and even violently opposed to equal-status interracial association that if an integrated interracial project were established by federal dictate (without other accompanying basic social
change) the interracial relations in the project would directly reflect
the tensions within the broader community.

c. The opportunity which the "change-experiences" provide for the
development of new sentiments. We have stressed the importance of
equal-status contacts as a means of breaking down prejudices, but
not all such situations allow equally well for the development of new
favorable sentiments. A situation which induces competition for scarce
goals is likely to promote negative rather than positive sentiments;
on the other hand, a situation which leads to the perception that only
through cooperative activity can any individual's goal be reached is
likely to result in cooperation toward common goals. The nature of
successful cooperative activity is such that communication, as well
as the development of positive sentiments among the cooperators, is
facilitated by it. (5, 6)

BIBLIOGRAPHY

1. Allport, G. W., and Kramer, B. M., "Some Roots of Prejudice," *Journal of Psychology*, 22:9–39 (1946).
2. Brophy, I. N., "The Luxury of Anti-Negro Prejudice," *Public Opinion Quarterly*, 9:456–66 (1946).
3. Chein, I., "The Problems of Inconsistency," *Journal of Social Issues*, 5:52–61 (1949).
4. Cox, O. C., *Caste, Class and Race*. Doubleday, 1948.
5. Deutsch, M., "A Theory of Cooperation and Competition," *Human Relations*, 2:129–52 (1949).
6. Deutsch, M., "An Experimental Study of the Effects of Cooperation and Competition Upon Group Process," *Human Relations*, 2:199–231 (1949).
7. Festinger, L., "Informal Social Communication" in *Theory and Experiment in Social Communication*. Univ. of Michigan, 1950.
8. Goldstein, R. L., "A Study of Interracial Practices and Attitudes of Negro Dentists in Nashville, Tenn.," an unpublished study, Fisk University.
9. Information and Education Division, U.S. War Department, "Opinions About Negro Infantry Platoons in White Companies of Seven Divisions" in *Readings in Social Psychology*. Holt, 1947.
10. Krech, D., and Crutchfield, R. S., *Theory and Problems of Social Psychology*. McGraw-Hill, 1948.
11. Lewin, K., *Resolving Social Conflict*. Harper, 1948.
12. Lewin, K., and Grabbe, P., "Conduct, Knowledge, and the Acceptance of New Values," *Journal of Social Issues*, 1:53–64 (1945).
13. Lindzey, G., and Rogolsky, S., "Prejudice and Identification of Group Members," *Journal of Abnormal and Social Psychology*, 45:37–53 (1950).
14. MacKenzie, B. K., "The Importance of Contact in Determining Attitudes Toward Negroes," *Journal of Abnormal and Social Psychology*, 43:417–41 (1948).
15. McCulloch, M. C., *Segregation: A Challenge To Democracy*. Fisk University, 1950.
16. Merton, R. K., *Social Theory and Social Structure: Toward the Codification of Theory and Research*. Free Press, 1949.
17. Murphy, G., *Personality: A Biosocial Approach To Origin and Structure*. Harper, 1947.
18. Murray, H. A., and Morgan, C. D., "A Clinical Study of Sentiments," *Genetic Psychology Monographs*, 32:3–149, 153–311 (1945).
19. Myrdal, G., *An American Dilemma*. Harper, 1944.
20. Newcomb, T. M., *Social Psychology*. Dryden, 1950.
21. Rose, A., "Race Relations in a Chicago Industry," an unpublished study, Univ. of Chicago, 1946.
22. Smith, F. T., "An Experiment in Modifying Attitudes Toward the Negro," in *Teachers College Contribution to Education*, p. 887 (1945).
23. Smith, M. B., "The Personal Setting of Public Opinion," *Public Opinion Quarterly*, Winter 1947–48, pp. 507–23.
24. Tolman, E. C., "There Is More Than One Kind of Learning," *Psychological Review*, 56:144–55 (1949).

A Note on "Differential Selection" of Tenants for the Two Types of Projects

"WHICH comes first, the chicken or the egg?" This is the problem which inevitably faces the social scientist who makes an *ex post facto* investigation such as ours. Did the attitudinal differences between the housewives in the integrated interracial and the segregated biracial projects exist prior to their residence in public housing and perhaps *cause* them to move into the one or the other type project? Or did the differences in attitudes *result* from their living in the different types of projects?

In Chapter IV we presented some reasons for believing that little differential selection occurred in the tenanting of the two types of projects we studied. We found little to support the possibility that the tenant population of the integrated projects had been less prejudiced initially than that of the segregated projects and considerable reason to think that the two populations had been essentially similar in their attitudes. Our reasoning, to recapitulate, was as follows:

1. As a result of the desperate need for housing among those eligible for low-income, public housing, so few who could get housing refused it that there was little opportunity for selection on the basis of attitudes. The rate of refusals was low — estimated as less than 5 percent (for all reasons, only a few of which are relevant to race) in both the New York and Newark authorities. In addition, voluntary move-outs, for all reasons, have been infrequent during the period about which we have data,[1] at an average annual rate of about 3 percent in Koaltown and of about 6 percent in Sacktown. Though

---

[1] These average figures are based on records covering 1944 through 1949 (data for the prior years were unavailable). They include voluntary move-outs for both Negroes and whites.

precise figures are not available for Newark, it is unlikely that they are any lower.

2. If, however, the prejudices of some eligible people were sufficiently strong to make them resist the lures of housing that is incomparably superior to that generally available to low-income groups, we should expect that they would reject equally the integrated inter-racial or segregated bi-racial projects we studied. All four projects are located in predominantly Negro neighborhoods; a prejudiced person could not ignore the pervasive "Negro" impression visually created by the neighborhoods of all four projects.

3. To a certain extent, the possibility in Newark (which did not exist in New York) of moving into an all-white project instead of into a bi-racial project might create more resistance in the prejudiced person to moving into a project containing Negro families than was the case in New York where there were only integrated projects. To the extent that this prevailed in Newark it worked in a direction contrary to our findings, i.e., it had the effect of bringing less prejudiced tenants into the Newark projects.

We have presented two types of evidence in previous chapters which also bear on the question. (1) In Chapter IX we presented data on the recollections of the housewives about their attitudes prior to moving into their respective projects. Our general finding was that the housewives in Sacktown reported having had less prejudice and the women in Koaltown more prejudice than was reported by the women in either of the segregated projects. There was no evidence from their recollections of differential selection due to the occupancy pattern per se. (2) In Chapters VI, VIII, and IX we presented analyses of the effects upon attitudes of various differences we found between the populations of the two types of projects. Our assumption in these analyses was that if differential selection occurred and the housewives in the New York projects were less prejudiced than Newark housewives prior to moving into public housing, this lesser degree of prejudice would be associated with certain types of previous experiences with Negroes, or with amount of education, or type of political belief, or religion, etc. The association of prejudice with these factors has been reported in other studies. Our analysis demonstrated that the differences in attitudes found to characterize the two types of projects cannot be attributed to differences in these factors.

Still another type of evidence is relevant to the question of differential selection.[2] During the course of the interview, we asked each

[2] We are indebted to Professor Gordon W. Allport for suggesting this analysis.

housewife: "When you made your application to move into ―――― (project), did you know that there would be colored and white families here?" If her reply was yes, we then asked, "Did you think that colored and white families would be living in the same buildings?"

Table 25 gives the percentage of housewives in each project who believed (1) that Negro and white tenants would live in the same buildings, (2) that Negro and white tenants would live in the same project but *not* in the same buildings, and (3) that the project was all white in composition and were surprised to discover its interracial character at a later date. It is quite clear from the table that the majority of white tenants in the integrated projects knew before filing their applications that they would be living in the same building with Negro tenants. Similarly, it is clear that the majority of white

TABLE 25. PERCENTAGES OF HOUSEWIVES WITH DIFFERENT EXPECTATIONS ABOUT THE OCCUPANCY PATTERN WHEN FILING APPLICATION TO LIVE IN THE PROJECT

Housewife's Expectation	Integrated Interracial Projects		Segregated Bi-Racial Projects	
	Koaltown (100)	Sacktown (85)	Bakerville (100)	Frankville (97)
Believed Negroes and whites would live in the same building	67%	74%	4%	7%
Believed Negroes would be in the project but in different buildings	10	7	72	57
Believed the project would be all white	23	19	24	36

tenants in the segregated bi-racial projects knew that they would share a project but *not* a building with Negro tenants. A sizable minority in all four projects did not know that the tenant population would be interracial: 23 percent in Koaltown, 19 percent in Sacktown, 24 percent in Bakerville, and 36 percent in Frankville. The percentages in this category were somewhat higher for the segregated than for the integrated projects.

We cannot, of course, say anything about the interracial attitudes of the housewives who held these three beliefs about the housing for which they were applying. It is possible, however — and it is on this assumption that we make the analysis to follow — (1) that only the white housewives who are least prejudiced would apply for housing knowing that they would share a building with Negroes; (2) that more prejudiced housewives would apply if they knew they had to share with Negroes only the project but not their building; and that (3) the most prejudiced would be found among the housewives who had applied in the belief that the project was all white.[3]

As we have already noted in Table 25, the majority of housewives in the integrated projects fall into category 1 (assumed to be the least prejudiced). The majority in the segregated projects fall into category 2 (more prejudiced). In addition, a somewhat higher percentage in the segregated than in the integrated projects fall into category 3 (most prejudiced). Taken together, these figures would lead us to expect, on the assumption of differential selection due to pre-project attitudes, a much higher incidence of prejudice in the segregated than in the integrated projects. This is, of course, what our findings show. In other words, if the assumptions made above about the correspondence between degree of prejudice and pre-application expectations about the character of the project are true, this correspondence might account for most or all of the project differences we have attributed to occupancy pattern.

The figures in Table 26 make it possible to check the validity of the assumptions in the above argument. The housewives in each project have been divided into three categories on the basis of their expectations with regard to the character of their project when they applied for admission, and the percentage of those in each category showing unprejudiced attitudes on each of four different attitude measures has been computed.

In terms of the assumptions we are examining, we should anticipate in each project and for the four projects taken together an increasing frequency of unprejudiced responses as we move from those respondents who did not expect to live with Negroes to those who knew they would live in the same building. Such a trend is found only in the case of attitude toward a policy of interracial housing for the city in general. For the remaining three measures no consistent differences appear.

In terms of the assumptions that differential selection was operating, we should also anticipate that housewives holding the same pre-application expectations would have similar attitudes in the four projects. We find, on the contrary, that regardless of pre-application ex-

[3] We make these assumptions, of course, realizing that they may not be completely valid. Thus, the women who fall into category 3 are, of course, not necessarily prejudiced. The fact that they did not withdraw their application or move out when they learned of the occupancy pattern might indicate selective factors at work. However, on the average, it is not unreasonable to assume that if selective factors were operating, then the women in category 1 are less likely to have been prejudiced than the women in category 3.

TABLE 26. PERCENTAGES AND NUMBERS OF HOUSEWIVES WITH DIFFERENT PRE-APPLICATION
EXPECTANCY WHO INDICATE HAVING
CERTAIN INTERRACIAL RELATIONSHIPS OR ATTITUDES

Attitude or Relationship	Expectation Concerning the Presence of Negroes											
	Integrated Interracial Projects						Segregated Bi-Racial Projects					
	Koaltown			Sacktown			Bakerville			Frankville		
	In Proj. and in Same Bldg.	In Proj. but Not in Same Bldg.	Not in Proj.	In Proj. and in Same Bldg.	In Proj. but Not in Same Bldg.	Not in Proj.	In Proj. and in Same Bldg.	In Proj. but Not in Same Bldg.	Not in Proj.	In Proj. and in Same Bldg.	In Proj. but Not in Same Bldg.	Not in Proj.
Have neighborly contacts with Negro women*	39% (67)	20% (10)	44% (23)	70% (63)	80% (5)	75% (16)	0% (4)	0% (72)	4% (24)	14% (7)	6% (54)	0% (35)
Have friendly feelings toward Negroes in the project†	39 (67)	30 (10)	57 (23)	65 (63)	33 (6)	44 (16)	0 (4)	9 (72)	13 (24)	14 (7)	4 (54)	3 (35)
Have favorably changed in attitudes toward Negroes in general‡	55 (65)	70 (10)	59 (22)	60 (62)	84 (6)	56 (16)	0 (4)	28 (71)	29 (24)	43 (6)	16 (55)	12 (84)
Favor an integrated interracial policy for the city**	58 (62)	20 (10)	39 (22)	58 (62)	40 (5)	31 (16)	25 (4)	3 (72)	4 (24)	14 (6)	4 (51)	3 (35)

* Here defined to mean having at least one type of contact (visiting, doing things for one another, shopping together, going out together) with at least one Negro woman. See Chapter V for further discussion of neighborly contacts with Negro women.
† As indicated by statements expressing desire to be friendly and neighborly with Negro tenants; see Chapter VIII for further discussion.
‡ See Chapter IX.
** As indicated by a recommendation of an integrated pattern in answer to a question about what policy the city should follow; see Chapter IX.

154

pectation the frequencies of unprejudiced response are much higher in the integrated than in the segregated projects. The frequencies of favorable attitude in the segregated projects range from 0 percent to 16 percent as compared to a range of 31 percent to 75 percent in the integrated projects. This is also true for "favoring an integrated interracial policy for the city." [4] If we limit the comparison to the housewives in each project who did not expect to live in the same project with Negroes we find in the segregated projects frequencies of favorable attitude ranging from 0 percent to 29 percent (considering A, B, C, and D in Table 26) as compared with a range of 31 percent to 75 percent in the integrated projects.

To sum up, we have examined a variety of evidence to determine whether differential selection on the basis of prejudice or differences between project populations in such factors as religion and education could provide an adequate explanation for the many differences in attitude we have found between the segregated bi-racial and the integrated interracial projects that we have studied. All of the evidence — the reports of the housewives themselves, the analysis of our data with factors other than the occupancy pattern held constant, the socio-psychological situation at the time of tenanting of the projects, etc. — is consistent in discounting the possibility that factors other than those associated with the occupancy pattern could account for these differences. This is not to deny that some differential selection may have occurred or that if it occurred, it spuriously enhanced some of the differences between the two types of projects. It is, however, a denial of the notion that differential selection (in the light of the evidence we have summarized above) offers a reasonable explanation of our research findings.

[4] Thus, even if we assume that prior attitudinal differences among the women with the various anticipations about the occupancy pattern does indeed affect their attitudes toward an integrated interracial policy, it is clear that the effects of the prior attitudinal differences are smaller than the effects due to the occupancy pattern.

Selection and Training of Interviewers

INTERVIEWERS were recruited from two sources: graduate schools in psychology and a graduate school of social work. Nineteen interviewers, eleven women and eight men, fifteen whites and four Negroes, were selected on the basis of previous interviewing experience, general maturity, interest in the research, and performance in the training period. Training groups were formed, and each group spent approximately twelve hours in training sessions. After hearing a thorough exposition of the scientific importance of the study, the specific purpose of each question, and an analysis of the content of the rating scales,[1] each interviewer obtained two interviews in an integrated housing project which was not to be studied. These practice interviews were then reviewed and discussed in the two training groups and individual problems were worked out. Throughout the period of data collection, the authors were in each of the housing projects to supervise the assignments and inspect the interviews as they were completed. The interviewers were systematically switched from project to project, so that all interviewers (except one who dropped out) interviewed in the two types of projects. To achieve maximum rapport with the housewives, the interviewing of white housewives was done by white interviewers and the interviewing of Negro housewives was done by Negro interviewers.

[1] Experience during the interviewing indicated that many of the rating scales were unreliable. They nevertheless served to sharpen the interviewer's sensitivities to inadequate responses to questions and to the need for further probings.

The Sampling Procedure

THE research design called for one hundred interviews with white housewives (that is, women customarily at home during the day) in each of the four interracial projects. A random selection of one hundred apartment numbers of white residents was made. Not less than two call-backs were made in the case of refusals and no answers. A substitution procedure, again using a random sampling, was followed where it was impossible to obtain an interview. Despite the fact that these women are constantly badgered by salesmen, the total refusals amounted to between 8 and 10 percent for the various projects; the majority of refusals occurred before the housewife had any knowledge of what the interview was to be about (i.e., the housewife would merely say, without opening her door, "Go away and don't bother me. I'm not buying anything.").

It is difficult to define precisely the characteristics of the universe from which we sampled. In terms of the sampling operation, however, they were the same for all four projects — women who, though not ill, tended to be at home during the day and who were sufficiently cooperative to be interviewed.

Statistical Tests of Significance

THOUGH the mathematical assumptions underlying the use of statistical tests of significance are not met by our data, in accordance with customary procedure and to provide a rough guide for the interpretation of data, routine statistical tests of significance were made on all comparisons of the two types of projects. To avoid burdening the reader, the statistical tests have not been presented in the text. However, it can be stated that any difference stressed in the text is statistically significant in the sense that it would not occur more than 5 times out of 100 by chance alone. In making the statistical tests, using standard procedures we computed the significance of the difference between percentages for each of the two matched pairs (Koaltown-Frankville and Sacktown-Bakerville) and then combined the resulting "p" values — when the differences between the matched pairs were in the same direction — to obtain the probability of the joint occurrences of the differences between the two pairs. The probabilities were combined according to the formula $M = -2$ Sum $\log_e p$, M being distributed in the form of chi-square with degrees of freedom equal to twice the number of probabilities being combined.

The Interview and the Rating Scales

The Interview

Interview # _____   Project _____   Interviewer _____

1. (a) How long have you been living in _____(Project)? Less than 6 mos.___;
Less than 1 yr.___; 1___ 2___ 3___ 4___ 5___ 6___ 7___ 8___.
   (b) Have you ever lived in any other apartment here? Yes___ No___.
   (If yes) Where? _____

2. Now that you've been living in _____(Project) for _____(q. 1), I wonder
if you'll tell me how you feel about it? _____
_____
_____

   (a) What do you like *most* about it? _____
   _____

   (b) What do you *dislike* most about it? _____
   _____

   (c) How about the neighborhood? What do you think of it? _____
   _____

   (d) How about living in a public housing project? _____
   _____

   (e) How about the apartment? _____
   _____

   (f) If you have any problems, is there anyone in management or anyone in the
   office that you can talk them over with? Yes___ No___. (If yes) Who?_____
   (Any remarks about management) _____
   _____

3. Where did you live before you moved into _____(Project)? _____
4. Why did you move from there? _____
_____

5. Before you moved into _____(Project), how did you feel about coming to
live here? _____
_____

   (a) What hopes did you have about living here? _____
   _____

   (b) What fears did you have about coming to live here? _____
   _____

6. What are your future plans: Would you like to continue living here, or, if you
could, would you like to move out and live someplace else? Stay___ Move out ___.
Why? _____
_____

159

Now suppose for a while that a good friend of yours has been offered an opportunity to move into _____(Project). Let's also suppose that she doesn't know anything at all about _____(Project) or anything about the people who live here. She's interested in finding out something about the different kinds of people that live here, how they get along together and how she'll like them. So she visits *you* and asks:

7. What are the people in _____(Project) like? _____

    Can you tell me more? _____

    (a) Are all of the people here like that? Yes__ No__. (If yes, go on to q. 8.)
        (If no) What kinds of people are like that? _____

        What kinds of people are *not* like that? _____

8. What (other) different groups of people live here? _____, _____, _____,
    _____, _____, _____.
    (a) What group do you belong to? _____

9. What about the colored people who live here? What are they like? _____

    (a) Can you tell me more about them? OR, Can you tell me something about
        them? _____

    (b) Are they pretty much the same as the white people who live here or are they
        different? Same__ Different__ Don't know__. (If Same or Don't know)
        Are there *any* ways in which they are different? _____

        (If Different) In what ways are they different? _____

    (c) Why do you think they're the same (or different)? _____

    (d) Are they pretty much the same as the other colored people who live in
        this part of the country or are they different? Same__ Different__ Don't
        know__. Why? _____
    (e) THEN YOUR FRIEND ASKS: Do you think that I'd like the colored people in
        _____(Project)? Yes__ No__ Don't know__. _____

    (f) THEN SHE SAYS: Suppose I move in, would I be likely to get to know any
        colored people in the project? Yes__ No__ Don't know__. _____

    (g) Where would I meet them mostly? _____
    (h) THEN YOUR FRIEND SAYS: You know I have two children; my girl is 14 and
        my boy is 9. What will it mean for them to live in a project where there are
        different kinds of people? _____

10. (FOR SECOND GROUP*) SUPPOSE YOUR FRIEND ASKS: What about the _____ who
    live here? What are they like? _____

   * The second group refers to either the Italian or to the Jewish group. The interviewers were asked to inquire about the Italian group unless the housewife or her husband was Italian. If the housewife or her husband were Italian, the interviewer was instructed to ask about the Jewish group.

(a) Can you tell me more about them? OR, Can you tell me something about them? _____

(b) Are they pretty much the same as the other white people who live here or are they different? Same___ Different___ Don't know___. (If Same or Don't know) Are there *any* ways in which they are different? _____

(If different) In what ways are they different? _____

(c) Why do you think they're the same (or different)? _____

11. (a) Out of every ten families in this project, about how many would you say are colored families? (Probe: 1 in 10, etc.) _____
(b) About how many would you say are _____ (second group) families?

12. How about you? How do you feel about living in a project like _____(Project) where there are colored and white families? _____

(a) What things *don't* you like about living in a project where there are families of different races? _____

(b) What things *do* you like about living in a project where there are families of different races? _____

(c) On the basis of your experience of living in a project where there are colored and white families, what plan do you think the city should follow in new projects? Do you think that colored and white families should be given apartments anywhere in the project no matter what their race is, OR do you think colored and white families should be allowed to live only in separate buildings in the project, OR do you think projects should be only all white or all colored? Anyplace___ Separate building___ Separate projects___.
Why do you feel that way? _____

(d) Since you've moved into _____(Project) have you come to like the idea of living in a project where there are colored and white families more___ about the same___ or less___? (Comment): _____

(e) When you made your *application* to move into _____(Project), did you know that there would be colored and white families here? Yes___ No___. (If yes) Did you think that colored and white families would be living in the same building? Yes___ No___ Don't know___. (Comment): _____

13. Can you remember what you thought colored people were like before you moved into the project? _____

14. How much have your ideas about colored people changed since you have lived in the project? _____

(If some change) In what ways have they changed? _____

(If some change) What do you think made you change your ideas? What experiences have you had while living here which caused you to change your ideas?

_____

15. (a) Are there any reasons why you think it might be better for you *not to have* much to do with the colored families in the project? _____

_____

    (b) Are there any reasons why you think it might be better for you to *have friends* among the colored families in the project? _____

_____

16. Are there any people or groups like relatives and friends who care one way or the other about whether you're friendly with colored families? Yes___ No___. (If no, go on to q. c.)

    (a) (If yes) Who are they? _____

    (b) (If yes) How do they feel? _____

    (c) How about your husband? How does he feel about your being friendly with colored families? _____

    (d) How about your friends in the project? _____

    (e) How about your friends outside the project? _____

    (f) What do the people on the management staff *really* think about it? _____

    (g) How about the colored people in the project? _____

17. (a) Have you ever lived near colored families before you moved into _____ (Project)? Yes___ No___ Don't know____. (If yes) Same block?___ Same neighborhood?___ Next door?___ Same building?___

    (b) I was wondering if you've ever worked on a job with a colored person who was doing the same kind of work as you? Yes___ No___ Don't know____. (If yes) Doing what?___ (Probe for relative status): _____

    (c) When you went to school, were there any colored children in your classes? Yes___ No___ Don't know____.

    (d) Have you ever had any friends who were colored before you moved into _____(Project)? Yes___ No___ Don't know____. (Comment): _____

One of the things that we're particularly interested in learning something about is how people get to know one another in a project like this.

18. (a) How many people in the project do you consider to be your close friends?

    (b) Will you tell me the five persons in the project you know the best? Where do they live?

Name	Same Floor	Same Stairhall	Same Building	Other Place	Negro	White
1. _____	—	—	—	—	—	—
2. _____	—	—	—	—	—	—
3. _____	—	—	—	—	—	—
4. _____	—	—	—	—	—	—
5. _____	—	—	—	—	—	—

    (c) How did you get to meet them? _____

_____

(d) Are any of them colored persons? Yes___ No___. (Comment): _____

(e) Are any of them _____(second group) persons? Yes___ No___.
(Comment): _____

19. (a) Do you usually call the women you know pretty well by their first or last names? _____

(b) How many women on this floor do you know pretty well? ___. Are any of these women _____(second group)? Yes___ No___ Don't know___. (FOR NYC): Are any of them colored? Yes___ No___. (Comment): _____

20. How many *other* women in the rest of the stairhall (hallway or entrance) do you know pretty well? ___. Are any of these women _____(second group)? Yes___ No___ Don't know___. (FOR NYC): Are any of these women colored? Yes___ No___. (Comment): _____

21. How many *other* women in the rest of the project do you know pretty well? ___ How many of these women are _____(second group)? ___ How many of these women are colored women? ___

22. How do you get to know women in the project? _____
_____

23. (a) Are there any differences in the way you get to meet the white women and the colored women in the project? Yes___ No___ Don't know___. (If yes) What are the differences? _____

(b) How about the _____(second group) women? Differences? Yes___ No___ Don't know___. (Comment): _____

24. (a) How many people *outside* the project do you consider to be close friends? ___
(b) Do you have more friends *inside* or *outside* the project? _____.

25. How many people who work here in the project do you know? ___
Who are they? _____

26. In general, would you say that the people here in the project are very friendly? Yes___ No___. (Comment): _____

(a) Are they more friendly or less friendly than the people in the neighborhood where you used to live? More___ Less___ About the same___ Don't know___.

(b) About how often do you go and just visit with the women here in the project, or do women come and visit you? More than once a day___ Once a day___ More than once a week___ Once a week___ More than once a month ___ Rarely___ Never___. (If any) About how many women do you visit with back and forth? ___
Do you visit back and forth with any of the colored women in the project? Yes___ No___. (Comment): _____

Do you visit back and forth with any of the _____(second group) women in the project? Yes___ No___. (Comment): _____

(c) Do you and the other women in the project help one another out, like taking care of one another's children___; shopping for one another___; helping one another when someone is sick___; or anything like that? _____

(If yes) Do you ever do any of these things with the colored women? Yes___ No___. (Comment): _____

     (If yes) Do you ever do any of these things with the _____(second group) women? Yes___ No___. (Comment): _____

(d) Do you and the other women in the project have any clubs like card clubs___; or sewing clubs___; or ironing clubs___; or any clubs like that? _____
_____

     (If yes) Are there any colored women in any of your clubs? Yes___ No___. (Comment): _____
     (If yes) Are there any _____(second group) women in any of your clubs? Yes___ No___. (Comment): _____

(e) Do you and the other women ever go out together, like go to the movies together___; or go shopping together___; or go down town together___? (Comment): _____
     (If yes) Do you ever do any of these things with the colored women? Yes___ No___. (Comment): _____
     (If yes) Do you ever do any of these things with the _____(second group) women? Yes___ No___. (Comment): _____

27. What kinds of things do you like to do in the free time you have, that is, during the time when you're not busy with the housework, cooking, cleaning, etc.? ___
_____

(a) What newspapers do you read when you have the time to read? _____
_____

(b) Do you go to any schools now, like night school, or attend any classes? Yes___ No___. (Comment): _____

(c) What was the last school you went to? _____

(d) Do you take part in any religious activities? Yes___ No___.

(e) What religion do you belong to? _____

(f) (If e is answered) How often do you attend services? Regularly___ Occasionally___ Never___.

(g) Do you belong to, or work with, any community organizations like the PTA, the Girl Scouts, political clubs, the Red Cross, or any groups like these? Yes___ No___. (If yes) Which ones? _____
_____

     (If g is answered yes) Have you ever been an officer in an organization like this? Yes___ No___.

28. (a) Do you take part in any (other) activities here in the project or belong to any clubs in the project? Yes___ No___. (If yes) Which ones? _____
_____

(b) (If yes) Have you ever been an officer in any of the clubs here in the project? Yes___ No___. (If yes) Which ones? _____
_____

29. How old are your children? Boys: ___ ___ ___ ___ Girls: ___ ___ ___ ___

30. Would you mind telling me how old you are? ___

31. (a) How about the children? Is there anything for them to do here in the project when they aren't in school? _____
_____
_____

(b) (If any activities) Do your children take part in any of the activities here? Yes___ No___. (If no) Why not? _____
_____

     (If yes) What activities? _____
_____

32. Do your children play with the colored children living in the project? Yes___ No___.

(a) (If yes) How do they get along together? _____
_____

(If no) Why not? _____

33. (a) Have you ever told your children about colored people? Yes___ No___.
    (b) (If yes) What did you say? _____

34. Does your husband have many friends in the project? Yes___ No___. (If yes)
    Are any of his friends colored? ___. (Comment): _____

35. What is your husband's occupation? _____

36. How much income would you *like to have* so as to be fairly well satisfied? _____

37. Generally speaking, how happy are you with your present state of affairs? _____

_____

38. What social class would you say that you and your family belonged to: Upper
    class___ Lower class___ Working class___ or Middle class___?

39. Now I'd like to find out how you feel about a few questions people are talking
    about these days. We want to find out how many women agree or disagree with
    these statements. Whether you agree or disagree with any statement, you can
    be sure that many other women feel the same way you do. I'll read these sen-
    tences and you just tell me whether you agree, are not sure, or disagree. (HAND
    HER THE CARD)
    (a) People with radical ideas shouldn't be allowed to become citizens of this
        country. Agree___ Disagree___ N. S.___.
    (b) Generally speaking, colored people are lazy and ignorant. Agree___ Dis-
        agree___ N. S.___.
    (c) Labor unions should become stronger and have more influence. Agree___
        Disagree___ N. S.___.
    (d) The Russians are so uncooperative that we are going to have to fight them
        sooner or later. Agree___ Disagree___ N. S.___.
    (e) In general, colored people can't be trusted. Agree___ Disagree___ N. S.___.
    (f) This country would be better off if no more foreigners were allowed to come
        here and live. Agree___ Disagree___ N. S.___.
    (g) There's something different and strange about colored people; it's hard to
        tell what they're thinking and planning or what makes them tick. Agree___
        Disagree___ N. S.___.
    (h) The government should own and operate all public utilities like railroads,
        gas, and electricity. Agree___ Disagree___ N. S.___.
    (i) If the common people were not allowed to vote, everybody would be better
        off. Agree___ Disagree___ N. S.___.

40. There are lots of different groups of people in the United States. People come
    from different countries all over the world to live here. (HAND CARD) Here is a
    list of some of the groups of people who live in the city. (READ) Chinese, Italian,
    Jewish, Negro, Puerto Rican, Irish, English.
    1a) If you were voting for mayor of the city (city commissioners in Newark)
        which of these groups would you like to have the mayor (commissioner)
        come from? _____
        (IF ANSWER TO FIRST PART OF QUESTION IS "I DON'T CARE," REWORD PART B
        TO READ, "ARE THERE ANY GROUPS WHICH . . . ETC.)
    b) Which of these groups would you *not* like to have the mayor come from?
    _____

    2a) If you were going to move into a new apartment house, which of these groups
        would you like to have living in the same building with you? _____

    b) Which of these groups would you *not* like to have living in the same building
       with you? _____
    3a) If you had a choice in sending your children to a school, which of these

groups would you like to have them go to school with? _____

b) Which of these groups would you *not* like to have your children go to school with? _____

4a) If you were in a card club or a sewing club, which groups would you like to have the women in the club come from? _____

b) Which of these groups would you *not* like to have the women in the club come from? _____

5a) If you were going to go out and work, which of these groups would you like to have the people you'd work with come from? _____

b) Which of these groups would you *not* like to have the people you'd work with come from? _____

41. We've talked about a lot of different things and I have just one more question to ask. What kinds of things do you think ought to be *changed* in order to have this project a better place to live in? _____

The Rating Scales Thumbnail Sketch
of Respondent

1. APPEARANCE: (Circle one in each group)
   tall — average — short   thin — average — fat   neat.— average — unkempt
   healthy — average — unhealthy
2. APPEARANCE OF THE APARTMENT: (Circle one in each group)
   orderly — average — disorderly   homey — average — cold
   poor looking — average — rich looking   clean — average — dirty
   needs major repairs — average — excellent condition
3. INTERVIEWING SITUATION: (Place check in the appropriate place on the line)

highly co-op	co-op	tolerant	slightly resistant	very resistant
1	3	5	7	9

completely understandable	mostly understandable	some difficulty understanding	considerable difficulty	very difficult to understand
1	3	5	7	9

Do you think the respondent's answers gave a pretty good picture of how she feels?

Yes	Probably	Not Sure	Probably Not	No
1	3	5	7	9

4. PERSONALITY: (Circle one in each group)

Sociability   *General Outlook*
sociable — average — withdrawn   happy — content — resigned — distressed

Emotional Level   *Attitudes*
mature — average — childish   rigid — persistent — flexible — fluid

Intelligence
superior — better than average — average — dull — borderline

Psychological Sensitivity
understanding — average — insensitive to people

Rationality
highly rational — average — pseudo rational — disorganized

167

5. ATTITUDE TOWARD LIVING IN THE PROJECT: (Check the appropriate place on the line)
a. Over-all sentiment

Likes project; no major qualifications	Generally likes living in project	Is ambivalent; likes some things, dislikes others	Generally dis- likes project	Strongly dis- likes project
1	3	5	7	9

b. Importance of sentiment toward the project on the person's general outlook on life

Highly important; colors his view considerably	Somewhat important	Not very important
1	5	9

c. What are the major determinants of this person's sentiments toward living in project?

POSITIVE	NEGATIVE
_____	_____
_____	_____
_____	_____

6. ATTITUDE TOWARD PEOPLE IN THE PROJECT:
a. Respect felt for Negroes in the project: (Place check in the appropriate place on the line)
Respect felt for people in the project generally: (Place (o) on appropriate place on the line)

Thinks highly of Negroes in project; without qualification	Generally re- spects Negroes living in project	Is ambivalent; respects certain things; feels they're inferior	Generally feels they're inferior	Strongly feels they're inferior
1	3	5	7	9

OR Circle X or Y below:
   X: Is indifferent to Negroes as a group; doesn't think about them.
   Y: Doesn't think of Negroes as a group; considers them as individuals.
b. Friendliness felt toward Negroes in the project: (Place check on the line)
   Friendliness felt toward people in the project generally: (Place (o) on the line)

Strong positive friendly feeling	Positive friendly feeling	Reserved: not friendly not avoidant	Somewhat avoid- ant feeling	Strong avoidant reaction
1	3	5	7	9

OR Circle X or Y below:
   X: Is indifferent to Negroes as a group; doesn't think about them.
   Y: Doesn't think of Negroes as a group; considers them as individuals.
c. Importance of attitude toward Negroes in the project in determining general attitude toward the project: (Place check in appropriate place on the line)
OR If attitude toward Negroes in the project seems to be determined by attitude toward the project: (Place (x) on appropriate place on line)

Highly important	Somewhat important	Not important at all
1	5	9

d. Determinants of feelings toward Negroes in the project:
(Indicate *rank order*: Place 1 in front of *major* determinant, 2 in front of determinant next in importance, etc.)
__ Past experience generally
__ Experiences in the project
__ Conformity to perceived general social standards
__ Conformity to perceived social standards in the project
__ Conformity to specific individual or group pressures (Specify group or individual: _____)

e. Consistency of rationale for feelings toward Negroes in the project: (Check appropriate place on the line)

Highly consistent; well organized	Fairly consistent	Loose organization; not thought out	No real consistency	Chaotic; major inconsistencies
1	3	5	7	9

f. Do respondent's feelings toward Negroes in the project appear to cause __ or to be the result __ of the rationales she offers for her feelings? Can't say__.

g. Determinants of action orientation toward Negroes in the project: (Indicate rank order: place 1 in front of major determinant, etc.)
__Sentiments; __Conformity to opinion of others; __Fear of consequences

7. ATTITUDES TOWARD NEGROES IN GENERAL
a. Respect felt for Negroes in general: (Place check in appropriate place on the line)

Thinks highly of Negroes in general; no qualification	Respects Negroes in general	Is ambivalent; respects certain things; feels they're inferior	Generally feels they're inferior	Strongly feels they're inferior
1	3	5	7	9

OR Circle X, Y, or Z below:
    X: Is indifferent to Negroes as a group; doesn't think about them
    Y: Doesn't think of Negroes as a group; considers them as individuals
    Z: Doesn't think of Negroes as a group; considers them the same as other people

b. Friendliness felt toward Negroes in general: (Place check in appropriate place on the line)

Strong positive friendly feeling	Positive friendly feeling	Reserved; not friendly, not avoidant	Somewhat avoidant feeling	Strong avoidant reaction
1	3	5	7	9

OR Circle X, Y, or Z below:
    X: Is indifferent to Negroes as a group; doesn't think about them
    Y: Doesn't think of Negroes as a group; considers them as individuals
    Z: Doesn't think of Negroes as a group; considers them the same as other people

c. Importance of attitudes toward Negroes in determining general attitudes toward democracy: (Place check in appropriate place on the line)
or If attitude toward democracy seems to be determined by attitude toward Negroes in general: (Place (x) in appropriate place on the line)

Highly important	Somewhat important	Not important at all
1	5	9

d. Determinants of feelings toward Negroes in general:
(Indicate *rank order*: Place 1 in front of major determinant; 2 in front of determinant next in importance, etc.)
___ Past experience generally
___ Experience in project
___ Conformity to perceived general social standards
___ Conformity to perceived social standards in project
___ Conformity to specific individual or group pressures (Specify group or individual: _____)

e. Consistency of rationale for feelings toward Negroes in general: (Check appropriate place on the line)

Highly consistent; well organized	Fairly consistent	Loose organization; not thought out	No real consistency	Chaotic; major inconsistencies
1	3	5	7	9

f. Do respondent's feelings toward Negroes in general appear to cause ___ or to be the result ___ of the rationales she offers for her feelings? Can't say___.

g. Determinants of action orientation toward Negroes in general: (Indicate rank order: place 1 in front of major determinant, etc.)
___Sentiments; ___Conformity to opinion of others; ___Fear of consequences.

h. If there are differences between the respondent's feeling toward Negroes in the project and toward Negroes in general, what is the rationale for the differences?

8. Any other comments: